Also by Lawrence Kutner, Ph.D.

Parent & Child: Getting Through to Each Other

Pregnancy and Your Baby's First Year

Toddlers and Preschoolers

Your School-Age Child

Making Sense of Your Teenager

LAWRENCE KUTNER, PH.D.

William Morrow and Company, Inc.
New York

It is the policy of William Morrow and Company, Inc., and its imprints and affiliates, recognizing the importance of preserving what has been written, to print the books we publish on acid-free paper, and we exert our best efforts to that end.

Library of Congress Cataloging-in-Publication Data

Kutner, Lawrence.
   Making sense of your teenager / Lawrence Kutner.
      p.   cm.
   Includes index.
   ISBN 0-688-10218-2
   1. Adolescence.   2. Adolescent psychology.   3. Parent and
teenager.   I. Title.
HQ796.K857   1997
305.23'5—dc20   96-33215
                                                        CIP

Printed in the United States of America

First Edition

1   2   3   4   5   6   7   8   9   10

BOOK DESIGN BY SUSAN DESTAEBLER

Acknowledgments

While some authors may be able to write a book entirely on their own, I am not one of them. Although the words are mine, I owe a debt of gratitude to numerous friends and colleagues in psychology, medicine, and journalism for their help and support.

Many of the ideas in this book spring from experience as a psychologist. Others come from the literally thousands of interviews I have done as a journalist, primarily for *The New York Times* and *Parents* magazine. It would have been impossible for me to have written this book without the countless researchers, clinicians, teachers, parents and others who have shared their wisdom with me over the years.

Several people deserve special recognition:

Al Lowman and B. G. Dilworth, my literary agents, have seen me through the past five books and have provided both insight and support when needed.

Toni Sciarra at William Morrow and Company took over as editor of the Parent & Child series midway through the project, and has used her editorial skills both elegantly and effectively.

Annie Murphy, Bill McCoy, and Kate Jackson, all of *Parents* magazine, have been just plain fun to work with. What a great group!

Violeta Stan, M.D., Ph.D., from Timişoara, Romania, has paid me the ultimate compliment of allowing her seventeen-year-old son Flavius to live with our family this year. He's a remarkable and talented young man. Living with him as I write this book (a serendipitous event) has provided me with a reality check.

Laurence Steinberg, Ph.D., of Temple University, has graciously shared his insights and very funny stories about adolescent development (including his own) over the years.

Richard M. Lerner, Ph.D., of Boston College and the editor of the *Journal of Research on Adolescence,* has been a good friend, a trusted colleague, and another source of great stories.

My colleagues at Harvard Medical School, especially Eugene V. Beresin, M.D., and Robert B. Brooks, Ph.D., have provided ongoing support in my efforts to combine psychology and communications.

Joyce V. O'Donnell offered her love and support when I very much needed it during my own stressful and turbulent adolescence.

As always, my cousins, Sol and Roz Kutner, have shown me the joys of being part of a supportive family.

My wife, Cheryl Olson (now, after years of hard work, Dr. Cheryl Olson), has been the mainstay of my life in so many ways. Her love and encouragement have given me the courage to test my own limits as a psychologist, journalist, parent, and husband. Just looking at her lets me know that I am truly a lucky man.

Finally I would like to give credit to my son, Michael, of whom I am more proud than I had ever imagined possible. He deserves my thanks for his love and patience, for I know how hard it must have been for him to wait for my attention the many times I said, "I'll be through writing in just a minute!" and then was not.

Contents

Acknowledgments..*v*

Introduction ....*xi*

1: THE IMAGE IN THE MIRROR 1
   Coping with the Changes..3
   The Timing of Puberty 4
   Gaining Perspective on Appearance...........................8
   When a Teenager Is Fat...9
   Helping a Child Lose Weight....................................12
   Eating Disorders..14
   Responding to Constant Dieting..............................15
   When Concerns About Appearance Are Valid 17
   Talking to Your Child About Cosmetic Surgery........19
   Teenagers with Disabilities.......................................21
   Helping a Chronically Ill Teen.................................24
2: PARENT-CHILD COMMUNICATION 26
   Arguing Productively 29
   Disagreements over Appearance................................31
   Dealing with Fashion Statements 33
   Motivation, Rewards, and Bribes..............................34
   Doing Unpleasant Tasks..37
   Disciplining Teenagers..38
   Teaching, Not Punishing...40
   Challenges to Religion...43
   Responding to a Religious Challenge......................45
   The Emotional Issues of Adopted Adolescents 47
   Helping an Adopted Teenager..................................50
3: EMOTIONAL DEVELOPMENT..52
   Rebels with a Cause..54
   Teenage Embarrassment..56
   Handling Embarrassing Feelings 58
   Depression in Adolescence..59
   If Your Teenager Seems Depressed 61

Leaving Home 62
   Deciding to Move Out 65
Runaways 67
   Dealing with the Threat to Run Away 69
The Driver's License 71
   Rules of the Road 75

4: FRIENDS AND PEER PRESSURE 77
   Understanding Friendships 80
Resisting Social Pressure 82
   Teaching Decision Making 84
Popularity 86
   Helping Your Child Be Liked 89
Shyness 90
   Helping a Child Gain Confidence 92
Sexual Harassment 93
   Helping a Child Who's Been Harassed 95

5: DATING 98
   The Timing of Dating 101
Preparing for the First Date 105
   Parents' Tips for Before That First Date 108
The Ritual of Prom Night 109
   Preparing for the Prom 111
When You Don't Like Your Teenager's Date 113
   Handling a Problem Date 116
Abusive Relationships 118
   Helping a Child Who's in an Abusive Relationship ...120
Sharing a Broken Heart 122
   Responding to the Breakup 124

6: RISKY BEHAVIORS: ALCOHOL, DRUGS, SMOKING, AND SEX 127
   Helping Avoid Drug Abuse 130
Decisions About Alcohol 132
   Avoiding Problems with Alcohol 134
The Lure of Smoking 137
   Helping a Child Quit or Not Start Smoking 139
Sex and Sexuality 140
   Talking About Sex 144

Sexually Explicit Material 146
   Reacting to a Teenager's Erotic Experimentation 148
7: MONEY, JOBS, AND CAREER ASPIRATIONS......................150
The Power of Money...152
   Paying the Piper...153
Where Credit Is Due...157
   Avoiding Credit Card Problems 160
Getting a First Job...162
   Helping with the Job Hunt 164
The Ideal Job..167
Problems on the Job..169
   Entering the Workforce 170
Trying on Careers for Size..171
   Channeling Career Aspirations 174
8: ON TO COLLEGE . . . OR PERHAPS NOT.........................177
   Cutting Through the Hype.......................................181
Taking a Break After High School 184
   Arranging for an Interim Program..........................187
The Emotions of the Freshman Year.............................188
   Responding to a Panicked Call 190
Visiting a Child at College 192
   Making the Most of a College Visit 194
Handling Potential Dropouts 196
   Listening to a Student's Fears 198
9: LETTING GO 201
Moving Back Home 202
   Guidelines for a Returning Young Adult 205
When Your Child's in Trouble.......................................207
   Offering Help...209
Competition 211
   Ending Painful Competition 212
An Ending and a Beginning..214

Index 216

Introduction

When I give speeches on child development across the United States and Canada, I find that the majority of parents who attend fit into one of two categories: those who have children under the age of three and those who have teenagers. Adolescence is a fascinating, frustrating, and confusing period not only in children's lives but in their parents' as well.

In this, the fourth and final book of the Parent & Child series, we'll take a look at some of what I consider to be the most interesting aspects of adolescent development. These are the topics about which I'm asked the most (and often the most poignant) questions by parents who see me in person or write to me at *Parents* magazine.

Here a few examples: What are the likely difficulties (and advantages) if your child reaches puberty ahead of his or her classmates? How can you motivate a teenager to do unpleasant tasks? What should you do if your child says he wants to live with someone else for a while? What pitfalls should you avoid if you dislike or distrust one of your child's friends? How can you help your child make decisions about using alcohol or drugs? What are the key elements of talking to a teenager about sex? What can parents do to help their children explore and choose a career? We'll explore these and many other aspects of what it's like living with an adolescent.

I've written in my previous books that childhood is like a symphony, with its underlying simple themes modified and recapitulated as the child matures. By adolescence these themes can be deceptively complex. Still, the simple melodies can be heard if you know how to listen.

That is what this book is all about. It is a look at what lies beneath the sometimes confusing and awkward behaviors of teenagers. It is an attempt to make sense of their actions and emotions by seeing the world from an adolescent's point of view. Finally, it is a chance to step back and look to see how we have changed (and will continue to change) as parents because of the growth of our children.

Although differences between boys and girls take on an added importance during adolescence, for the most part I have used the pronouns *he* and *she* at random and without prejudice. In those situations where the sex of the child is important for understanding a behavior or selecting a response, I have stated so.

This is not a book with magic solutions to problems. Publishers send me many such books to review, few of which live up to a shadow of their promise. My fundamental premise is that parents know their children more thoroughly than anyone else—even if there are moments when it feels as if our children are strangers. This book will give you some insights and, perhaps more important, some specific tools both to understand your teenage children and to help you develop your own custom-made solutions to problems that arise.

Two key elements to creating successful solutions are your attitude and knowledge. For years psychologists and other "experts" have warned parents that adolescence is, of necessity, a time of emotional turmoil. We now know that such generalizations are ill founded. Most teenagers get through this period of their lives with little of the dramatic Sturm und Drang that filled the experts' dire predictions.

But parents' expectations of such upheavals have occasionally led to problems. First, parents who braced themselves for alienation from their teenagers may have unintentionally and paradoxically triggered it. Second, some parents dismissed their children's true cries for help as little more than growing pains, thereby missing the opportunity to offer aid when such help was desperately needed.

You can avoid these problems by understanding what lies beneath your teenage children's attitudes and behaviors. You need to know why your thirteen-year-old doesn't want his friends to see you drop him off at their homes (and why you shouldn't take it personally). You need to understand why your teenage daughter is arguing with you more often (and why you should feel proud rather than resentful).

Finally, you need to keep your perspective—especially in times of stress. That's where a sense of humor can be one of the best tools a parent can have. It's most effective when you're able to laugh at yourself. Remember that life with teenagers is an adventure. Hang on and enjoy the ride!

Making Sense of
Your Teenager

1

The Image in the Mirror

I am fearfully and wonderfully made.

—PSALMS 139:14

For most adolescents, the mirror is both a comforting friend and a taunting enemy. They are drawn to its reflection, even if they dislike or worry about what they see. What they see mostly is change.

Adolescence—especially during the time around puberty—is punctuated by important and profound changes that mark the physical transition to adulthood. It is a transition that simultaneously comforts, confuses, and frightens many teenagers. It is as if their bodies are no longer their own. They are occupants of a new space, and are no longer sure of their physical boundaries.

A few weeks ago I spent several days with a thirteen-year-old boy who vividly showed the all-too-common clumsiness that accompanies an adolescent growth spurt. I watched as he entered a storage shed on his great-grandmother's farm and bumped his head on the low doorframe. He had ducked to avoid it, of course, but only as much as he'd needed to in the past. The resultant bruise on his forehead showed how his awareness of the size of his body was out of sync with his new height.

Later that day, as we walked side by side, he kept bumping into me. At first I thought I might be crowding him or that he was upset about something. But it soon became obvious that he simply no longer knew where his body stopped. He had grown wider than his mental image of himself.

Many teenagers become preoccupied with the shape of their ears, the size of their nose, or the predictable weight gain that accompanies puberty. It's normal for older children and teenagers to become concerned about real or imagined problems with how they look. Still, it's important to realize that their own feelings of attractiveness may have little to do with more objective measures of beauty. We can see the beginnings of this early on.

Very young children pay little attention to how they look. By the time they're in preschool, however, they've become aware of their culture's standards of beauty and of how they measure up. There's also a striking difference between girls and boys on this matter. According to research by Dr. Seymour Fisher at the State University of New York Upstate Medical Center in Syracuse, who studies body image in adults and children, by the time they're five years old, girls rate their bodies as less attractive than boys do.

This becomes a critical issue as children approach puberty. Acceptance by their peers and not standing out in a crowd become increasingly important. Much of a teenager's self-image is rooted in her appearance, which may be changing dramatically.

Indeed, early adolescents may pass through a phase of excruciating self-consciousness. Trivial things—at least to the eyes of a parent—may become a source of embarrassment and concern. Are her fingers the right shape? Is there something wrong with the color of her eyes or the shape of her ears?

Coping with the Changes

Those children who handle puberty best are often the ones who know the most about what's going on and what to expect. The awkwardness that accompanies adolescence makes the topic a difficult one for them to discuss, even though they may crave information about the changes they're undergoing.

Here are some ideas that may help:

- Don't tease your children about how they're changing. This appears to be a particular problem when fathers tease their daughters about things like breast development or putting on weight. While the intent may be good-natured banter, adolescents are especially sensitive to what's happening to their bodies and are likely to interpret such teasing as a sign that there's something wrong with them. Look for ways to celebrate the changes they're undergoing without embarrassing them.

- Share some of your own memories of going through puberty.[1] Children this age often feel that they're the only ones who've felt so clumsy, frightened, or emotionally overwhelmed. By hearing your stories, they can gain perspective and feel comfortable asking you questions.

- Pay attention if your child suddenly stops changing physically. This is particularly important for girls, who may feel tremendous pressure to stop the weight gain associated with puberty, especially if they're dancers or involved in other activities in which an angular figure is highly valued. If a girl's pubertal development seems to stop or reverse itself, that may be a sign of an eating disorder. (I'll discuss this further later in this chapter.)

The Timing of Puberty

On average, girls in the United States show the first signs of reaching puberty (usually a change in their breasts) when they're approximately ten and a half years old. Menarche (the first menstrual period) arrives about eighteen months after those first changes. Among boys, the first sign of puberty is usually the development of pubic hair, which appears, on average, a few months after their eleventh birthday.

---

[1] It's often best if the parent who's the same sex as the teenager does this. If you're in a single-parent family and your child's of the opposite sex, you may wish to have another family member or a close friend raise these issues.

Average ages are only useful as broad guidelines, however. As any visit to a seventh-grade class will show, there are tremendous natural variations in the age when children reach puberty, and in the pace at which they progress through the stages of maturation. There is seldom anything biologically wrong with children who are a few years ahead of or behind their peers.[2]

Still, the physical changes of puberty can be disconcerting to adolescents, especially if they appear out-of-step with their peers. For boys, reaching puberty early can be a social advantage. Their extra size, weight, and strength increases their athletic performance, which gets them extra positive attention from their peers. Conversely, a boy who reaches puberty later than his peers may feel socially inadequate until his body more closely matches those of his classmates.[3]

In most Western societies at least, girls tend to show reactions to early and late pubertal development that are opposite to those of boys. Studies by Dr. Jeanne Brooks-Gunn at Columbia University have found that girls who reach menarche in the fifth grade are more likely to be depressed than their peers, and more upset about the changes in their bodies.

Part of the distress early-maturing girls feel appears to come from comparing themselves to the idealized female body shape they see in the mass media. Physical attractiveness among women has historically been associated with a rounded shape, breast development, and other signs that differentiate the mature woman

---

[2] It's a good idea to have your child checked by a pediatrician if you don't see any pubertal changes at all in a girl by age twelve and a half or in a boy by thirteen and a half. While the vast majority of these children are perfectly normal medically, they may need extra emotional support and an explanation of what's happening (and not happening) to their bodies while they wait to catch up.

[3] It's important to remember, however, that a mature-looking twelve-year-old who's passed through puberty early still thinks and acts much like a prepubertal child of the same age. While the larger child may *look* more like an adult than his peers, we shouldn't expect adultlike judgment and behavior from him.

from a child. The current archetype of an attractive and desirable woman, as portrayed in North American and Western European magazines, however, is someone who is young, exceedingly thin, and more angular than rounded—in essence, little more than a prepubescent girl displaying an adult sensuality.

The same holds true in movies and on television, especially those produced in North America. Those films and television programs aimed at adolescents may make matters worse by distorting the real world. The teenagers who populate the big and small screens are almost always blemish-free and slender. Seldom do their ears stick out or their chins recede. Their noses can, at worst, be described as "cute."

Those teenagers who stand out physically—the ones with the thick glasses or acne—are likely to be foils for the main characters rather than heroes themselves. The problems of the thin blondes are portrayed as serious; the problems of the fat brunettes are trivial or, worse yet, funny.

While adults understand that the teenagers shown in films and television programs aren't typical, the adolescents watching those screens often do not. By comparing themselves to this new group, many teenagers feel even more convinced that they're fat or ugly.

Since the first sign of puberty in a girl is often weight gain, girls who mature ahead of their peers usually see themselves as less attractive than they had been.[4] One study by Dr. James C. Rosen at the University of Vermont surveyed three thousand adolescents about their bodies and eating habits. He found that while the majority of the boys were trying to gain weight, two thirds

---

[4] One notable exception was a study on early-maturing girls in Berlin, which found that they saw themselves as more attractive than their peers. The reason for this is unclear, although it may be that a more mature body type is highly valued rather than feared among the women in that city.

of the girls were trying to lose it. Although the majority of the boys who said they were dieting were obese, the majority of the girls who were trying to lose weight were at *or below* the normal weight for their sex and age. (I'll have much more on obesity and weight loss later in this chapter.)

Girls who reach puberty early—especially those who have their first menstrual period prior to their eleventh birthday—may be at risk for a variety of psychosocial problems. The change in their physical appearance often leads them to spend more time with older adolescents of both sexes. This makes them more likely to engage in early sexual activity as well as other behaviors for which they are not emotionally ready.

Dr. David Magnusson of the University of Stockholm has found that early puberty among girls has at least a temporary effect on other important psychosocial areas as well. His studies have shown that at age fourteen years and five months, early-maturing girls were more than twice as likely as late-maturing girls to have been drunk at least once, and nearly six times as likely to have been repeatedly drunk. The early-maturing girls were also more likely to use other drugs, to get into fights, and to engage in petty theft.[5]

---

[5] Keep in mind that, as with all such studies, he's describing risks within a population, not predicting the behavior of an individual girl who reaches puberty early. The best way for parents to use this information is to recognize that an early-maturing girl needs extra guidance and support because she's statistically more likely than her classmates to face a range of social problems earlier than her peers do.

Gaining Perspective on Appearance

If your child comes to you with concerns about how she looks, you should take that as a compliment. It shows that she feels secure enough in your relationship to trust you with this potentially painful and damaging information. It may be tempting to dismiss her concerns with comments like, "Oh, your nose is just fine!" Don't, for she will probably interpret your intended reassurance as a sign that you don't really care.

Instead, begin by acknowledging the intensity of her emotions. ("I can see that you're very upset. Tell me what's bothering you.") This gives her permission to continue and lets her know that you're willing to listen.

Here are some other things to consider:

- Dig beneath the surface of your child's complaints about how she looks. For example, ask her what she thinks her concerns mean. Sometimes young adolescents believe that having large ears or a birthmark means they'll never have any friends. Remember that a complaint about a physical "defect" is often an attempt to talk about an underlying issue, such as a problem with a friend or a concern about sex. If you just talk about appearance, you may miss the real problem.

- Don't single out your child for special treatment. This happens most frequently if the teenager is overweight and the parents insist that he eat different food from the rest of the family. This makes the child feel like even more of an outcast. A better approach would be for the entire family to change to a more healthful diet.

Keep in mind that eating and weight loss are the child's responsibility. If a parent tries to control her child's weight, that turns eating into a larger battle for independence and autonomy. That is a battle the parent is destined to lose.

- Look at other areas of your relationship with your child. Parents are sometimes overly critical of their children, giving them a general message that they're not up to snuff. A child may deal with this message by talking about problems with his body.

- Help your child gain a better sense of perspective. Remember that adolescents may feel that no one else has ever felt the way they do. Talk about your own experiences and feelings when you were an adolescent. That lets your child know that he's not the only person to have felt this way, and that he can survive this.

When a Teenager Is Fat

From a historical and even a current global perspective, it is quite a luxury to worry about a child who is overweight. To many people, especially those in third-world countries, it is a concept as bizarre as worrying about having too much money. For most generations and in many areas of today's world, having a few extra pounds of flesh on your bones is a sign of prosperity and fertility.

But all of that has changed, especially in economically developed countries. Concerns about heart disease have supplanted worries about obtaining adequate nutrition for survival. To many of today's teenagers, the female nudes painted by Rubens a few hundred years ago would appear fat and unattractive. Even Marilyn Monroe, who epitomized sexuality and sensuousness in America of the 1950s and 1960s, might be considered obese.

To be labeled as fat by a parent carries with it an additional burden for a child. Parents who believe that their teenagers are overweight and who try to help them lose the extra pounds often stir up resentments in both generations. For children, and especially for teenagers, losing weight is more a matter of emotions than of calories. The refrigerator and the dinner table quickly turn into battlegrounds. Food becomes the focus of most conversations between the children and their parents. Teenagers begin measuring their self-worth and attractiveness in terms of pounds and inches of fat.

"I nagged him," recalled a mother of an overweight teenager son. "I watched what he ate and died inside every time he ate an extra cookie."

The hyperbole in her description of her feelings about her son's eating habits is so common that few people would notice it. Still, it is quite telling. Food and weight bring out the most primitive of emotions: "I would kill for a piece of chocolate." "I don't dare let anyone see me until I lose another ten pounds." Although the people who say such things[6] would freely admit that they're exaggerating, even young children get the message that food and weight are associated with very intense and perhaps frightening emotions.

For some parents, having an overweight child is a sign of their own failure. Yet they may have difficulty acknowledging their feelings of anger, guilt, or embarrassment about having a fat child. Food and weight become the focus of the family's relationship.

A social worker I know, who directs a weight-loss program, recalled two parents who came to her office with their teenage daughter. Both parents were physicians. They told the social worker that if they couldn't get their daughter to lose weight, they might as well hand in their medical diplomas. The daughter, who heard the comment, received a very clear message about her weight: It was the only thing about her that mattered in the eyes of her parents.

Adolescents have two characteristics that make it harder for them than for adults to lose weight: They're impulsive and they're terrible at delaying gratification. In other words they don't have good self-control. They'd rather eat now and feel bad than not eat or delay eating.

Almost all the parents who accompany their teenagers to weight-loss programs have tried nagging, bribing, threatening, and cajoling their children into losing weight. Nothing seems to help. Parents get angry. Children withdraw. Parents feel guilty.

---

[6] I must admit that both my wife and I have made the chocolate statement.

Children feel embarrassed. The problems may be particularly acute when the parents remember being teased or ignored because they were overweight adolescents themselves.[7]

Nagging a child about losing weight is like playing a slot machine. Although there's no long-term success, every so often you get what you want. It's those occasional reinforcements that make the habit so hard for parents to break.

Other parents become food police, constantly monitoring and judging what the child eats. Yet children consistently report that they feel as if their parents are judging *them,* not their behavior. You're a good boy if you eat an apple. You're a bad boy if you eat apple pie.

Setting up this kind of power struggle is the kiss of death to an effective weight-loss program. If you set up a lot of restrictive rules, teenagers will respond to you by eating. If they're angry at you, they'll eat the foods you said they shouldn't. A better approach is to make choosing the right foods to eat the teenager's responsibility. That way it's less likely to be used as a tool to express rebellion or anger against you.

Helping a Child Lose Weight

Perhaps the primary mistake parents make when they have an overweight child is focusing exclusively on that child's weight. That gives the message "I don't love you the way you are. You'll have to change in order for me to love you."

---

[7] The mother I quoted at the beginning of this section told me that she had been overweight when she was fifteen. Her parents had nagged her and had even tried to bribe her—one dollar for every pound she lost, with a bonus of ten dollars for every ten pounds. It didn't work. Still, she tried doing exactly the same thing with her son.

Paying attention to other assets such as intelligence or social skills can make it much easier for a child to lose weight. Weight loss is a slow process, often taking six months or longer—an unbearably long time for an adolescent. A teenager who receives praise and recognition for successes is less likely to seek negative attention by cheating on a parent-imposed diet.

Here are some other ideas that may help:

- Keep track of how often your conversations with your child revolve around food. If most of your talks are about weight, or if the first thing you ask your child when he comes home from a party is "What did you eat?" that's a tip-off that something is wrong.

- Saying things like "You'd be so pretty if you were only thinner," while well-intentioned, are really quite devastating to a child's self-esteem. It undermines the emotional foundation they need to help them lose weight.

- Pay attention to whether the things you say to your children actually change their behavior. Parents say useless things to their children all the time, such as "You shouldn't be eating that ice cream!" You know that's true. Your child knows it's true. Saying it again and again won't help.

Eating Disorders

When teenagers look in the mirror, the reflection they see is usually a bit distorted by their fears and expectations. It's not simply a concern about ears that stick out or a nose that looms large, but with the overall shape of their bodies. Some worry that no one will see them as attractive unless they change themselves dramatically.

Perhaps nowhere is this more true than for those children who have an eating disorder. Forty years ago few physicians saw a single patient with anorexia or bulimia during their years of medical school. Now all they have to do is visit a typical high school.

There's growing evidence that parents should pay close attention to their children's body image and dieting habits, even if those children are not starving themselves, or bingeing and purging. While parents and physicians have grown more sensitive to these signs of anorexia or bulimia,[8] they often overlook less dramatic, socially approved behaviors that can also lead to both physical and emotional trouble.

Adolescents' worries about how their bodies are shaped, and their unrealistic expectations of how they should look, have grown so common that parents and health professionals accept them as normal. Dieting has become synonymous with wanting to stay healthy, even though it often has the opposite effect. Eating disorders have become plot devices for television movies, as if they had always been common conditions.

---

[8] According to Dr. David Herzog, a child psychiatrist at Harvard Medical School who specializes in eating disorders, 2 to 4 percent of girls develop anorexia and/or bulimia during adolescence. Only 5 to 10 percent of teenagers who have eating disorders are boys.

Research by Dr. Maryse Richards at Loyola University in Chicago found that those girls in the eighth and nineth grades who said they were concerned about their weight were more likely to have lower self-esteem, were less happy, spent less time with friends, and spent more time alone than those girls who were not worried about their weight. (This pattern did not hold true for boys, however.)

For teenage girls, this may be a matter of popular culture fighting biology. Gaining weight and changing body shape are normal and healthy aspects of puberty. Yet the images they see on television and in movies and magazines lead them to feel that any weight gain is a sign not only of unattractiveness but of failure.

Responding to Constant Dieting

A child who's significantly below her normal weight and who continues to diet needs specialized medical treatment, as does a child who's bingeing on food and then vomiting. But for the majority of teenagers who are dissatisfied with how they look, there are some things that parents can do to help.

- Talk about issues that may be behind the child's focus on weight or shape. Remember that adolescence contains periods of both social and physical awkwardness. A child who reaches puberty or has a growth spurt ahead of or later than her peers may feel very self-conscious, at least for a while.

If your child tells you she's too tall or too fat, ask her what she thinks that means. Does she feel she is unattractive? Is she worried about what others think? Often, just putting those thoughts into words, combined with some gentle guidance and reassurance from you, will help a teenager get a better perspective on her attractiveness.

You should become concerned if your child thinks that the shape of her body means she's less worthwhile as a person. If that's the case, seek professional help.

- Think about your own adolescence. Children are very sensitive to their parents' emotions, even when the parents are unaware that their feelings are showing. If you had trouble with your own weight when you were young, you may be transmitting that anxiety to your children.

- Examine your feelings about how you look as an adult. Your reassurances will have little credibility if you're of reasonable weight but are dieting yourself. Be careful about modeling unrealistic concerns about your own weight and appearance.

Also, talk to your child about common phrases like "You can never be too rich or too thin," or "One moment on the lips, a lifetime on the hips." How literally does she believe such words? Help her get a better sense of perspective.

When Concerns About Appearance Are Valid

Usually a child's cry of "I'm ugly!" signals little more than a need for emotional support and reassurance. The self-deprecation that is common toward the end of elementary school and in junior high school is a response to temporary feelings of rejection and despair. But there are also times when complaints that "my ears stick out," "my chin is too weak," or "my nose is so embarrassing" are based on reality.

All children want to be accepted by their peers. Many of the criteria for social acceptance among adolescents are physical, which is why young teenagers are so concerned with having the "right" clothes and hairstyles. (They become more comfortable being different as they enter later adolescence.) The bump on a child's nose that seemed small at age twelve may look like the largest thing in the mirror at fourteen, especially if none of your child's friends have bumps on their noses.

Children's complaints about their looks can be acutely distressing for parents. Parents see their children, in part, as reflections of themselves, and often overlook their children's minor flaws just as they overlook their own. Your long-standing conflicts about your own appearance can be rekindled when your upset child responds to your reassurances by blurting out, "But I have *your* nose!"

Most of the time simple words of comfort and assurance are enough to lift a distressed child's spirits. Because it is easier for a child to focus on a physical problem than to risk discussing the more complex and confusing emotions of adolescence, letting him know you love him despite what he sees as the flaws in his appearance can give him the courage he needs to address what's really bothering him.

For some children, however, cosmetic surgery can do a tremendous amount of good, both psychologically and physically. According to the American Society of Plastic and Reconstructive Surgeons, only about 4 percent of all cosmetic surgery is performed on children under the age of eighteen, but those operations account for 16 percent of rhinoplasties ("nose jobs") and 9 percent of chin augmentations.

If teenagers have a healthy and realistic set of expectations about undergoing cosmetic surgery, the change in their appearance can help them become more sociable and outgoing. They tend to feel better about themselves in general, not just about their appearance. But if they have unrealistic expectations about the results—especially if they feel the change in how they look will instantly make them more popular—they may develop more problems if those expectations do not materialize.

Having a child who wishes to undergo cosmetic surgery can put parents in an emotional bind. It's difficult to know when just a few reassuring words are enough to satisfy a teenager, or when changing the child's appearance may be best. One thing is clear, both from formal studies and from the individual experiences of plastic surgeons: The psychological consequences of cosmetic surgery tend to be much worse when the idea of undergoing the surgery comes from anyone except the child.

In fact, one of the plastic surgeons I interviewed for a newspaper column on this topic said that the first thing he asks is whose idea it was for the operation. If it's a parent's idea, he refuses to do it. If it's the child's idea, he said he's more likely to consider it.

But even a child's enthusiasm for cosmetic surgery is not

enough to determine whether such an operation is appropriate. Children under the age of twelve are generally unable to understand what cosmetic surgery involves, even after it's carefully explained to them. They expect to wake up and find that everything has changed and that there is no pain, bruising, or swelling.

The age of the child also affects whether a particular operation is appropriate. It's generally a bad idea to perform cosmetic surgery on parts of the body that are still growing. An obviously receding chin in a thirteen-year-old might be much less apparent in another few years. If it is augmented too soon, it might look too large when the child is a young adult.

Ears reach 80 to 90 percent of their adult size by age five or six. The nose reaches its final adult size around age thirteen in girls and fifteen in boys. The chin does not mature until age eighteen in girls and twenty-one in boys. And growing into those ears or that chin may be more a matter of mind-set than of head size.

Talking to Your Child About Cosmetic Surgery

Undergoing surgery of any type can be a touchy subject in many families. Cosmetic surgery brings with it additional emotional baggage. Here are some things to keep in mind, either when giving your child reassurance about his appearance or when discussing cosmetic surgery:

- Don't simply disagree with your child. Even if you think your child has the world's cutest nose, keep your appraisal to yourself. Remember that he may really be worried about other things, such as social acceptability. If you say his concern about his nose is ridiculous, it will seem as if his emotions in general don't matter to you and would be best kept hidden.

Instead, begin by acknowledging that he's upset. Let him know that you can see that this is important to him, but that you love him no matter how he looks or what he feels. If something else is beneath his complaint, that may give him the reassurance he needs to begin addressing that underlying problem.

- Take your time. Cosmetic surgery for a child or adolescent is not something you should agree to at once. Remember that one of the best predictors of the psychological success of plastic surgery is the consistency of the child's complaints about his looks. It's best to wait until a child brings it up several times over a period of years.

- Ask yourself if your child tends to stick with new things or becomes easily frustrated. Adolescents who are poor candidates for cosmetic surgery often have had trouble deciding on other things related to their appearance. Think about whether your child frequently changes eyeglasses or hair colors to try out different looks without any long-lasting consequences. If that's the case, she'll probably not be happy with the results of cosmetic surgery.

- Find out your child's expectations of surgery. Don't just talk about physical appearance, but about how your child thinks he will feel about himself. Why will he feel different? How will his friends react? Why will they react that way?

It's important to find out how realistic your child is about the results. As I stated earlier, those teenagers who expect large social changes to stem from the cosmetic procedure ("Lots of kids will like me when I have my new nose") tend to be poor candidates.

Also, children whose self-esteem is focused on fashion and appearance may have unrealistic expectations for the effects of cosmetic surgery. In some ways it's similar to those children who buy a heavily advertised pair of athletic shoes or team jacket because they believe those things will lead to an immediate and dramatic improvement in their performance. While owning a fashionable item may help a child become accepted by his peers, he will not be popular unless he has the necessary social skills as well.

Teenagers with Disabilities

Adolescence often brings special problems and stresses to children who have chronic diseases, such as asthma or kidney failure. Their illnesses may make them feel like outcasts at a time when they most wish to fit in with their peers. Even a visit to a fast-food restaurant can be acutely embarrassing to an adolescent who can't eat the same things as his or her friends.

The teenage years are marked by ambivalent and awkward struggles for independence. Having a chronic disease puts a different twist on that adolescent's need to separate. Whether the illness thwarts a child's emotional growth or enhances it depends in part on how parents handle the situation.

It's important to remember that children who have a chronic illness or other disability have been more dependent on their parents than those children who are generally healthy. That makes any rebellion appear more dramatic.

This is especially true for parents who blame themselves for their child's problems or who have taken total responsibility for their child's medical regimen. An adolescent's natural desire for greater independence and self-reliance can frighten these parents. What if he has an asthma attack or forgets to take his medicine? What if he needs me and I'm not there?

While all parents lose (and gain) something when their child becomes an adolescent, those parents who have become emotionally overinvolved in the care of their child face an even greater loss.

Perhaps the best way to help children who have chronic illnesses handle the normal strains of adolescence is to get them more involved in caring for themselves when they're younger. What appears to be most important is not the amount of responsibility the children have but the feeling of control that comes from helping to make decisions about their day-to-day lives.

According to research by Dr. Gerald P. Koocher, the chief psychologist at Boston Children's Hospital, those children who felt they had the fewest choices and the least control over their lives were least likely to comply with their physicians' instructions about how to handle their disease.

One reason for Dr. Koocher's interest in this topic is that he has a teenage daughter who developed diabetes when she was eight years old. She learned how to give herself insulin injections soon after her diagnosis—although she wanted her parents to give them to her at first. Slowly she's taken increasing responsibility for her own care, although for several years she wanted to have one of her parents in the room when she gave herself an injection or tested her blood.

To help his daughter handle the social pressures she was beginning to feel as a teenager, Dr. Koocher encouraged his daughter to talk to her friends about her condition. He also sent her to a summer camp for diabetics. Both helped her focus on her similarities to other children instead of her differences from them, which in turn will help her handle the more intimate emotional relationships she'll develop with her friends over the next few years.

Intimacy can be a stumbling block for disabled or chronically ill teenagers, especially if they haven't been forthcoming about their medical problems. Such teenagers may worry about becoming close to their friends for fear they'll be rejected because they're different.

One approach to helping prevent such problems is to encourage a chronically ill adolescent to confide in her best friend about her disease and its treatment. That best friend can act as the child's advocate in social situations that might otherwise be awkward. For example, an adolescent whose diet is restricted will feel more comfortable going with friends to a fast-food restaurant if at least one of those friends supports her decision not to eat what everyone else is having. That way she can get the acceptance and friendship she so desperately (and naturally) craves, without putting herself at as much risk of rejection.

Helping a Chronically Ill Teen

The most important thing to remember about adolescents who have chronic diseases is that first and foremost they're adolescents, not patients. If you expect these teenagers to become invalids, they'll become invalids. But if you think of them as normal children who have a disease, they'll have a much more normal life. As a pediatrician I know once put it, "Their brains don't rot because their pancreases aren't working!"

If your teenage child has a chronic illness, here are some other things to keep in mind:

- Concentrate on empowering your child. If, for example, your child has to adjust her medication according to what she eats, don't do the calculations for her. Instead, help her figure out what her options are. In other words, help your child explore choices and make informed decisions regarding her treatment instead of just telling her what to do. This will give her a greater feeling of control over her life.

- Don't minimize the social aspects of your child's condition when she reaches adolescence. Remember that being socially accepted is extremely important at this age. Help her see that she's not a bad, weak, or inferior person because something about her is different.

  Acknowledge your child's anger and frustration about her disease. Don't try to deny those feelings.

Let your child ventilate them as a step toward coming to better terms with her emotions.

- Don't expect your child's behavior to be consistent. While occasional erratic behavior is a hallmark of adolescence in all children, it can be especially worrisome to parents of a teenager who's ill. It's normal for a teenager and even for an adult to regress a bit during times of stress, such as a hospitalization. If you accept these variations in behavior and apparent maturity without turning them into a big deal, they will pass more quickly.

- Don't give your child more responsibility for her own care than she can comfortably handle. While you want your child to become more involved, it's important that you move slowly so that she doesn't feel abandoned or rejected. You don't want to make her feel that taking responsibility for her own care is one more thing an adult is forcing her to do.

2

Parent-Child Communication

An unpracticed observer expects the love of parents and children to be constant and equal; but this kindness seldom continues beyond the years of infancy.

—SAMUEL JOHNSON (1709–1784)

The parent-child relationship takes on a different tone during adolescence. A teenager's natural drive toward independence is sometimes in conflict with a parent's hope for family harmony. A teenager's desire to explore more complex and abstract issues—to exercise and test the developing areas of his brain just as he strengthens and tests his developing muscles—often means that he questions his parents' beliefs about such matters as religion and justice.

These incidents can offer parents tremendous insights into how their adolescent children are maturing, and a glimpse of what they may be like as adults and, perhaps, as parents themselves. But making the most of the changes in the parent-child relationship during adolescence means that parents, too, must change. It is often necessary to look below the surface of the child's questions, arguments, and desires to discover the fundamental processes going on. Doing so can be tremendously rewarding for both generations.

Although they may at times act as if they have little use for their parents' opinions and guidance, teenagers are desperately seeking help in understanding the world from their new perspective. Their bubble of bravado is thin and fragile. They are watching and listening very closely to their parents and the other important adults in their lives, even if they don't wish to admit it.

In this chapter I'll explore several areas that show different aspects of this changing parent-child relationship. We'll begin with conflict, since that is sometimes the most obvious sign of change (and growth) within a family.

While constant battles are a sign of deeper problems, a reasonable amount of parent-adolescent conflict is not only normal but helpful as well. One way that teenagers learn who they are is by bumping up against others who have different beliefs. It allows them to sharpen their ideas and more clearly define their points of view.

Researchers have found that the frequency of parent-child battles has two predictable and related peaks. The first occurs during the "terrible twos," when children are struggling to demonstrate their physical and, to a lesser extent, emotional independence from their parents.

The second peak occurs around the time of puberty. These struggles also revolve around independence and control. Of course, the arguments with adolescents are different from those with toddlers or even school-age children, for teenagers can use them to test their newly improved but imperfect skills at reasoning.

This is the time when children realize that their parents aren't always right. Many parents find the discovery of that flaw threatening, for their children are now more likely to question and challenge them. Most frustrating for both parents and teenagers is when their arguments repeat themselves leaving everyone feeling angry and dissatisfied.

Feeling caught in a rut with your arguments is often a sign that parents and adolescents are paying too much attention to the wrong things, or misunderstanding what the fights are really about. Battles that seem to center on friends or curfews are often reflections of much deeper issues, such as privacy and trust.

That's why focusing simply on how late your child is allowed to come home after seeing a movie, for example, misses the point. Also, if parents or children are anxious about sexuality or intimacy issues, they may deal with anxieties by arguing even though the heated exchanges in those arguments aren't necessarily about those topics.

Repeated arguments can also be a sign that the child feels neglected or ignored. Starting a fight can be the most effective way to get parents to pay more attention, even though the emotional cost is high. Here, however, the topics of the arguments form a different pattern than those brought about by normal rebellion. The subjects of the disagreements and challenges will tend to be different each time, reflecting an unmet need for attention that has nothing to do with the individual conflicts.

Repeated fights can also be a sign that parents are giving unclear or inconsistent messages about the limits they're trying to set. Their children have learned that, although the stated house rule is that they must be in bed at ten o'clock, if they argue about it, they can probably stay up an extra hour. They are reinforced for having the argument.

The parents, who quite naturally dislike these battles, are reinforced for their behavior as well. If they give in to their child's demands, the arguing stops—at least until the next time the child wants something and thinks having another argument is the most expedient way to obtain it.

Here the goal is to let the teenager have greater autonomy, but not feel that she has to yell and scream to get it. Holding regular family meetings can help avoid this problem, as long as the children get to help develop each meeting's agenda. Remember that the real objective of both the meetings and the arguments isn't to win your battles but to help teenagers and younger children learn productive ways of solving problems. Too often during family fights the participants get locked into attaining their short-term goals and forget about their more important long-term objectives.

Arguing Productively

Although it may be comforting to know that many of the battles parents have with their children are both normal and predictable, it doesn't make them any more pleasant. This is especially true if the arguments become repetitive and don't seem to get anywhere. If that's the case in your family, here are some ideas that may help:

- Identify what you're really arguing about. That's not as simple as it sounds, since it may have little to do with the words you're using. It's often useful to talk to other parents of children the same age as yours to see if you can discern a fundamental pattern.

Many of the repeated battles with adolescents are over superficial issues. But the underlying theme is often something more basic, such as who's in charge or how parents should recognize the changes in their children.

- Make a list of what you're fighting with your child about. If no pattern emerges, try writing down the situation in which the arguments occur. Ask your child to do the same thing.

    You may find that the battles usually start when you're questioning your child's self-reliance by asking whether she has finished her homework or whether she has a class project ready. If that's the case, work on ways that she can demonstrate her abilities so that you don't have to question them as often.

    Better yet, ask your teenager to help solve the problem. You might say something like "I know you hate it when I ask you if you've finished your homework. What would be a better way for me to reassure myself that you're staying on top of your assignments?" With your help, she might come up with any number of approaches, from showing you her work occasionally to agreeing to answer your question only on Mondays, Wednesdays, and Fridays.

What's most important is that you're showing her that you recognize her emotions and that you're willing to change. That helps her do the same for you.

- Ask yourself if you're giving your child mixed messages. Has your child learned that you dislike arguing so much that you will back down under provocation? If that's what's happening, help your child learn more appropriate and effective ways to get what she wants, such as negotiating or presenting a reasoned but low-volume argument. To teach those skills, you will have to use them yourself and avoid exhibiting other behaviors you don't want her to enage in, such as sarcasm and name-calling.

    Remember that when parents are very angry, children don't hear parents' words, only their emotions. Your goal is to turn down emotions so that the message gets through.

Disagreements over Appearance

Battles between adolescents and their parents over dress and appearance seem to be a tradition passed on from generation to generation. Teenagers' insistence on the privilege of choosing how they look and what they wear serves a very useful purpose in their emotional and social development. But in many families, those developmental issues sometimes get lost among the details of pierced ears or spiked hair.

It's important to remember that adolescents are going through immense bodily changes over which they feel they have no control. One way of taking control of how they look is through their style of dress. While they may not be able to dictate the size of their breasts or whether they have acne, they *can* control what they wear and the other ways in which they choose to adorn themselves.

Adolescence is also a time for testing independence. The bravado with which some teenagers announce their autonomy belies their underlying normal anxieties about making that difficult transition from child to adult. Their choice of fashion reflects this emotional conflict. Although their clothes are meant to set them apart from both adults and younger children, their choices are usually remarkably similar to the things their peers wear. There is safety and comfort in this apparent contradiction. The transition to independent thought and responsibility is made easier when the child still feels a part of a group.

One useful guideline is that unless your child is going to do something dangerous (e.g., body piercing with unsterilized instruments) or permanent (getting a tattoo), you should encourage her to express herself through her appearance. At the same time, you should discuss with her the possible consequences of her decisions.[1]

Choosing a strikingly different hairstyle is a common way of asserting control and emphasizing the teenager's differences

---

[1] This can lead to an absolutely fascinating series of discussions dealing with not only your child's appearance, but her increased awareness of equity and justice. While it isn't "fair" that shaving half her head, having a large ring through her nose, or wearing dirty and torn clothing will limit the after-school jobs she's likely to obtain, it's true. This is an opportunity for her to explore her more sophisticated skills at empathy and to understand the potential positive and negative ramifications of her choices about how she looks.

from her parents' generation. A psychiatrist friend of mine recalled his initial reactions a few years ago when his daughter, then fifteen years old, announced that she wanted to dye a streak of her hair purple. My friend was outraged and dead set against it—until he recalled his own shoulder-length hair during the 1960s.

For many adolescents, having the right to make these choices is more important than the choices themselves. It is a signal of their parents' recognition of the teenagers' maturity, and a sign of how their relationship is changing. Discussions about fashion can be an excellent means of clearing the way for talks about these more important underlying issues.

Dealing with Fashion Statements

Knowing that it's normal to express individuality doesn't make it much easier when your daughter announces that she wants to shave her head or your son states that from now on he'll wear only black. The key to resolving problems you have with your children's fashion choices is to gain a sense of perspective. Here are some specifics:

- Choose your battles carefully. Allow your children to make both choices and mistakes in this area. Wardrobes can be changed and hair will grow back.

  Deciding when to stand your ground is critical. It's much more important to set standards and limits on sexual behavior, drug use, and schoolwork than on dress and hairstyle.

- Focus your discussions on the underlying issues. Don't get bogged down in whether it's "right" to have spiked hair or to wear a half-dozen earrings— battles you're sure to lose. Instead, use the situation as an opportunity to understand what these things mean to your child, what your child wants to accomplish by looking like this, and perhaps to find a compromise position.

- Explore the possible consequences of their decisions with your children. This is especially important if their choices are permanent or potentially dangerous, such as getting a tattoo. In addition to talking about benefits and risks, discuss how long it might take to recover from a mistake.

  This is a good opportunity to demonstrate how an adult thinks about this type of decision. Go over timelines for what they're considering and how long it might take to change back. For example, your child might not realize at a gut level that if she shaves her head, it will take *months* for her hair to grow back.

Motivation, Rewards, and Bribes

Most parents would agree that it's generally better to reward children for doing what you want than to punish them for avoiding unpleasant tasks such as finishing their homework or cleaning the cat's litter box. Yet psychologists who study motivation say it's not that simple. In fact, sometimes parents and teachers actually worsen the problem they are trying to cure when the rewards they offer are perceived by adolescents as bribes.

There's a big difference between doing something for enjoyment (intrinsic motivation) and doing the same thing for a reward (extrinsic motivation). A teenager who wants to play the guitar so that she can have fun with her friends in a band will joyfully practice for hours. The improvement she hears in her technique and the scope of the songs she can play are more than enough reward to motivate her to spend long hours practicing chords and riffs. A classmate who has little interest in music will look for ways to avoid even a few minutes of practice, even if her parents have promised her a prize for learning a new song.

Does this mean that your teenager should only do the things she finds enjoyable, or that you have to look for ways to make most of her activities fun? Absolutely not! That's an impossible and inappropriate task. Rather, you should take the type of motivation into account when you're trying to understand or change your child's behavior.

Children who are motivated extrinsically approach a task differently than those who find it interesting or fun. A teenager who's enjoying herself will view difficulties and mistakes only as temporary setbacks to be overcome. A child whose motivation for a behavior is extrinsic will tend to give up when she encounters problems or is told that she's doing something wrong.

Offer effects are more subtle. Numerous studies have shown that if a reward can be gained only by doing an undesirable task, the task tends to become even less attractive. Let's say you've told your fourteen-year-old daughter that she'll be allowed to watch television only if she finishes her mathematics homework.

The girl will tend to enjoy doing the math problems less than if she hadn't been offered the reward or if she had simply been told that she could do her homework and watch some television.

That approach also encourages the child to shift her focus from the task (doing the homework) to the reward (watching television). She'll try to get the reward with the least amount of effort, probably by rushing through the math problems. A child who's told that she should clean her room because that's one of her duties as a family member will tend to do a better job of it than one who feels she's doing it mostly to get her allowance.

Teachers fall into this trap as well. Telling a student who doesn't like science that she'll get a bonus for doing her homework will not increase her enjoyment of the subject. In fact, the emphasis on the reward may lead her to dislike science even more.

The size of the reward intended to motivate a child also appears to have an effect, but not the way many parents believe. Large rewards tend to draw the child's attention away from the task. Studies have shown that children who are offered a large reward—an item worth fifty dollars to one hundred dolllars, for example—tend to enjoy a task less than children who are offered a small reward, such as a slice of pizza.

Offering a large reward also tells children that, ultimately, their parents are taking responsibility for seeing that a task is done. Not only is the value of the work passed by—be it a school project or family chores—but the children become more dependent upon their parents for the next reward.

Doing Unpleasant Tasks

There's a difference between helping a child develop certain values, such as a sense of responsiblity, and getting a task done, such as taking out the garbage. Getting the task done is the easy part. Here are some ideas that can help with the important, underlying issues:

- Let your children know that you are aware of and respect their opinions. After all, no one really enjoys taking out the garbage. By stating that you realize it's sometimes a smelly and messy job, you're letting them know that their feelings are valid but that they must still do their part. If you try to convince them that something is interesting or enjoyable when it isn't, you're saying that their feelings don't count.

  The same holds true for doing homework. Acknowledge that sometimes it isn't fun and that it might be more pleasant to talk on the telephone or watch television, but make it clear that this doesn't mean they should avoid their school assignments.

- Avoid offering rewards for things that are out of your child's control. If you say you'll give a child a certain amount of money for each A on his report card, the child will have no reason to keep working hard if he feels he will never get that grade.

  Instead, focus on the activity you want your child to do, such as studying or getting his papers handed in on time. Involve your child in figuring out a study schedule. That makes him more likely to follow through than if you simply imposed some rules.

- Look at your own behavior. You can hardly expect a child to clean up his room if your room is a mess. Ask yourself if you're doing the things you ask your child to do. If the answer is no, you may have to be the first one to change.

- Don't offer large rewards. Remember that doing so tends to foster dependence on the rewards and to make the task even less attractive. The rewards you offer should be symbolic so that they're not the reason for doing the task. They're simply an acknowledgement of work well done.

Disciplining Teenagers

The emotional, physical, and intellectual changes of adolescence have a profound effect on how parents discipline their teenage children. With young children, parents are mostly benevolent dictators. We can, by and large, decide whom our children will see and what they will do. While young children will test how serious their parents are about those limits, they will rarely question their parents' right to set them.

All that changes with adolescence as parents learn that the old dictatorial approaches to discipline no longer work. No more will children accept everything their mother and father say simply because they are the parents. The children may be physically

larger than the parents, and unresponsive to a previously successful threat of withholding dessert.[2]

At the same time, adolescents often lack the maturity or sense
of perspective they need to make some important decisions that
affect their safety and future. They crave the security and structure that come with dependable family rules, while bristling at
the constraints those rules place on their independence.

Some parents, especially those whose identities are tightly
wrapped up with those of their children, have difficulty making the adjustment to disciplining adolescents. Often these
parents were very successful at handling younger children,
but become frustrated when their authority and decisions
are challenged.

Other parents fight their teenage children's natural and appropriate need for independence. They may try to pull their kids
closer because they're afraid of losing control over them. But the
harder a parent pulls a teenager in, the harder that child is likely
to jerk away.

The frequency with which adolescents challenge adults is
largely a reflection of their growing intellectual abilities, not a
sign of rebelliousness or disrespect. Teenagers can become intense moral philosophers, using their newfound skills at sophisticated abstract thinking to argue over fine points that, only a year
or two earlier, they would have missed.

The sophistication of teenagers' emotions, however, may not
keep pace with the changes in their intellectual skills. Although

---

[2] One mother I interviewed for a newspaper column told me that her tried-and-true punishment for
her stepson when his behavior became intolerable—sending him to his room—ceased working when
he became a teenager. She finally realized that his room now contained a television, telephone, computer, and stereo system. Of course he wasn't upset to be sent there!

their ability to reason is much more sophisticated than it had recently been, teenagers sometimes fall into a pattern of thinking usually associated with preschoolers: They have difficulty seeing the difference between *doing something* bad and *being someone* bad.

As a result, they may describe politicians or other public figures with whom they disagree as "evil," as if the difference in values defined the other person's worth and personality. Similarly, they may insist that their favorite rock stars are "wonderful" people because they like their music—and may quickly discount any negative reports of their idols' behavior.

This shift toward simplistic thinking in the face of intellectual growth can show up at home as well. Teenagers can be tenacious in their insistence that they did not stay out past curfew—maintaining that they returned on time or asserting that their parents had given them permission to stay out late—even though the parents met them at the door when they returned and did not remember granting any special privileges.

Teaching, Not Punishing

For parents to use discipline effectively, we must remember that it is not the same thing as punishment. Discipline shares the same Latin root as the word *disciple*. The core of discipline is teaching.

Here are some suggestions that will help you both reach and teach your adolescents:

- Set limits on your children's behavior, not their emotions. Adolescence can be a time of emotional upheaval. Help your children understand, for example, that although they may feel angry and express that anger, they should not strike out at someone because of it. Remember that you should accept your teenager's feelings, but you don't have to accept her behavior.

- Don't abdicate your authority. One reason your teenager may challenge your authority is to assure herself that you will be there no matter what she does. At the same time, you should share with your teenager the reasons behind your decisions that affect her, and listen to her point of view on those topics as well.

  Keep in mind, however, that while you should explain your rationale, you don't have to persuade her that you're right. Your child has to learn to live with the fact that the two of you can disagree but that you're still the parent. Although she may seem peeved, your child actually finds this clear role definition reassuring.

- Give your teenager increasing responsibility along with privileges. Teenagers need to know that you recognize their growth. While granting a child new privileges, such as being able to go out after school with her friends for a pizza, is one way of offering that recognition, so are responsibilities.

I've found it useful to pair the two, requiring an added (and appropriate) responsibility for each new privilege. When possible, the two should have a natural connection. ("You may borrow the car on Saturday, but you have to return it with the gas tank full.")

- Make your rules and expectations as explicit as possible. This by itself will cut down on the number of battles with your children. Adolescents will test those rules anyway, of course. But it's less stressful and destructive to your family if the boundaries you establish are clear and reasonable.

  For example, "You have to be back home, inside the front door, by ten-thirty P.M." lets your child know exactly what your expectations are. If instead you'd said, "Be sure to be home at a reasonable hour," your child will probably interpret those expectations differently than you will. In fact, many teenagers will feel obligated to test exactly how late "a reasonable hour" is.

- Admit your mistakes. Frustrated parents sometimes mete out inappropriately severe punishments in the heat of the moment ("You're grounded for the next six months!") and then worry that if they change their minds, their children will see them as weak.

  Many long-term punishments, such as restricting a child's social activities for more than two weeks, are ineffective because they tend not to be enforced. Even if they are enforced, after a few weeks the children will often forget why they are being punished and will simply become resentful.

If you've been unreasonable in your punishment because you were very angry, admit that to your children and correct the punishment. This is, after all, the sort of behavior you'd want from your children as well. If you refuse to admit your mistakes and to change your position, your children will feel that they have to act that way as well.

Correcting your mistakes doesn't undermine your authority, it adds to it. Your children will think more highly of you than if you had stuck to your guns even though you realized you were wrong. Just don't do it every time.

Challenges to Religion

A few years ago, I interviewed a psychologist who described the trouble he'd caused at home when he was thirteen years old and living in New York City. He'd violated the Sabbath by riding the subway to see his school basketball team play in the city championship. His parents, who were Orthodox Jews, were quite upset.

The psychologist was seventy-five years old at the time I spoke to him. His own teenage rebellion was so important to him that it was one of the clearest and most important memories he had of his adolescence.[3]

---

[3] Like many teenagers, he eventually decided that his approach to religion would vary slightly from that of his parents. As he put it, "I feel very good about the values and traditions of our religion, but how I give expression to those values and traditions is different."

One of the most common ways adolescents and even young adults rebel against their parents is by challenging their religious views. Their rejection of aspects of the family religion can be very upsetting to parents. Yet psychologists who study religion and members of the clergy who work with young people say this type of rebellion is often healthy, especially if religion is central to the family's life.

In fact, it may be a cause for concern if an adoolescent adopts the parents' religion without giving it any thought or shaping it in his own way. In those families, religion is more likely to be used as a way of controlling behavior than of questioning what life's all about.

When an adolescent announces that he will no longer go to Mass or Hebrew school, or will not attend Sunday services after being confirmed, he dramatically calls attention to himself as newly mature and independent. His declaration is sure to bring a reaction from his parents, and can be a way of broaching other topics or problems that he feels uncomfortable addressing directly.

Rejecting a religion is an easy way to challenge much broader issues, such as fmaily relationships and value systems. It can be especially painful for parents because it implies a rejection of a worldview, of values, and of special occasions when a family gathers together.

While teenage rejections of religion may be dramatic, they are seldom permanent.[4] Just as an adolescent may speak with great conviction about becoming a physician one week and a lifeguard the next, this may be a way of trying on new and different adult

---

[4] Because of their maturational differences and different emotional needs, rejections of religion by young adults are much more likely to be long-lasting or permanent.

roles. Indeed, it's common for teenagers to sample other religions, sometimes with great but short-lived fervor.[5]

Occasionally, adolescents will take a different approach in order to demonstrate their maturity. There's also turmoil in families when children become more devout than their parents. That's another kind of rebellion.

Responding to a Religious Challenge

It's difficult to react calmly when your child talks about rejecting your religion. But responding too dramatically will often lead to more rejections. Instead, consider the following:

- Remember that rebellion is normal. Although the apparent content of the teenager's rebellion may focus on religion, it may be part of a more general process of questioning and exploration. Ask yourself if your child is really rejecting your religion or is demonstrating his independence.

  Teenagers are struggling to master complex and abstract issues, including religion. They may also suddenly become interested in political or social programs because they can now analyze what's going on in more sophisticated ways. This growing sophistication on your child's part allows you to talk to him about which aspects of your religion he's ques-

---

[5] I attended Quaker meetings for several years when I was in high school after I was involved in a work project run by the American Friends Service Committee. It was a safe way to rebel and explore on several different levels.

tioning or rejecting: the rituals, the structure, or the fundamental beliefs.

- Try not to back your child into a corner. Children are often looking for adults' recognition that they're no longer completely dependent on their parents. For example, don't insist that your child attend your church, since your demand will likely make him feel you're treating him like a young child and will increase the intensity of his rejection.

  Instead, use his refusal as an opportunity to talk about alternatives. Those might include visiting other houses of worship, reading about different religions or looking for new ways of expressing his beliefs.

- Don't assume that all rejections of religion are the same. There's a distinction between those who are moving away from a religion as part of a rebellion and those who reject the family religion because they're seeking something else. Adolescents who are looking for a different type of spirituality may find it by reexamining their own religion from a new perspective.

- Don't assume that rebelliousness toward religion is a major problem. A certain amount of confusion over religion is a good thing. It reflects the teenager's new cognitive skills.

  Talking to your child about differences of opinion shows that you recognize his increasing matu-

rity. It also gives him permission to raise other matters that may be troubling him.

- Respect your child's decision. Although you should
  feel free to disagree and to express your reasons for
  disagreeing, your underlying tone should be respect.
  That will help prevent differences in religious beliefs
  from driving a wedge between you.

The Emotional Issues of Adopted Adolescents

The subject of adoption is often ignored in books about older
children.[6] This is a shame, since adolescence can be an especially
difficult time for adopted adolescents. Their normal teenage striv-
ing to become less involved with their family and to establish
themselves as individuals can bring forth surprising and sometimes overwhelming feelings. It can also make adoptive families
face aspects of their history and relationship that they have
avoided.

This is not to say that adolescence is bound to trigger a crisis
for adoptive families. Rather, being adopted can change the ways
in which teenagers perceive and interpret some of their normal
developmental drives.

Issues of separation, sexuality, and identity permeate the nor-

---

[6] This is a topic that I find both personally and professionally fascinating. I was adopted as an infant;
as a psychologist I've done research on adoption; and for the past five years I've been on the board
of directors of Adoptive Families of America. Finally, my wife and I have been the nonadoptive "temporary" parents of a teenager from Romania—the son of a friend and colleague of ours—who has
been living with us.

mal course of adolescence. For adopted children, those issues may have potentially frightening implications. The struggle during adolescence is particularly acute because the child is trying to break away from her family. But a teenager who's been adopted may feel more cautious because she's been given away by one family already.

That puts adolescent adoptees in an emotional bind that often has little to do with their history or how well they have been integrated into their family. They may worry that something is inherently wrong with them that led to their being put up for adoption. They may wonder whether they will be rejected again if they are successful at separating from their parents.

Often those thoughts are so threatening that children cannot face them directly. Instead, they deal with their feelings symbolically through their words and behavior.

For example, a psychiatrist I work with who specializes in adoption issues told me about a thirteen-year-old boy he was treating who had been adopted at birth and who had suddenly begun acting coldly toward his father. The boy had started having fantasies that his biological family might come for him in helicopters at any time. He told his father, "If I get close to you, then I would lose you."

Coming to terms with their burgeoning sexuality may also cause more problems for adopted than for nonadopted adolescents. As they start to think about their ability to have children of their own, adopted teenagers often begin to wonder about their own biological parents and the decisions that went into giving up their child.

One of the feelings many of these children have—which is often unfounded—is that their birth mother was sexually promiscuous. That may lead them to be more concerned than non-adopted children about their normal sexual urges. They worry that if they separate from their adoptive parents, they may become sexually promiscuous as well. It is a concern that they are unlikely to express directly.

Identity is another issue that presents special problems to adolescent adoptees, especially if their parents come from another race or culture. Often, these children feel awkward or out of place in both the society in which they were born and the one in which they were raised.[7]

These additional stresses are reflected in the relatively large proportion of adopted children who are referred to psychiatrists, psychologists, and counselors. Studies have found that adopted children are two to five times as likely to be referred for mental health treatment as nonadopted children.

But these figures may be misleading. It's unclear what proportion of those differences reflects the children's behavior, and how much shows the adoptive parents' familiarity with the mental health system and willingness to seek outside professional help. By the time adoptees reach their twenties and thirties, this difference in use of mental health services disappears.

---

[7] In the United States and Canada this is a particularly complex issue with Native American children, who usually have little chance of having contact with their culture of origin and may see inaccurate and mostly negative images of it through the mass media.

Helping an Adopted Teenager

If you have adopted children, here are some ways to make their adolescence less turbulent:

- Talk openly to your children about their adoption. Pretending that it doesn't matter will probably make your child more anxious instead of more open. Children worry that they may hurt your feelings if they raise the issue. Make sure that your child knows that it's safe to talk about adoption with you. Acknowledge that being adopted can be different. It's normal to be angry or confused about it at times.

- Expect some conflict over your relationship with your children during adolescence. Adopted teenagers sometimes say things like "I don't have to listen to you. You're not my real parents."

  Keep in mind that nonadopted adolescents say similar things to their parents as well. It's more a function of adolescence and the need to separate than of the adoption.

  At the extreme, some adopted adolescents will behave as if they want you to throw them out. This is a way for them to test whether their home really is a secure base for them. Still, it's a good idea to get some professional help if their behavior is this extreme.

- Let your children know that you won't reject or abandon them. This is the answer to the question that worries them most, even if they don't ask it directly. Communicate that your home is where they really belong and are welcome, even if they fight and misbehave.

3

Emotional Development

Young men, in the conduct and management of actions, embrace more than they can hold; stir more than they can quiet; fly to the end without consideration of the means and degrees.

—FRANCIS BACON (1561–1626)

A pediatrician I know told me how a distraught couple had brought their thirteen-year-old son to his office, convinced that the recent changes in the boy's behavior indicated he had a brain tumor. The boy's personality was different, they said. His use of language had grown odd. He had become uncharacteristically rebellious. After evaluating the boy, the physician sat down with the parents and explained that their son was perfectly healthy. All the symptoms they'd described were actually signs of a normal adolescence.

The teenage years are a time of flux, as children take awkward steps toward becoming adults. The physical changes of puberty, such as growth spurts and sexual maturation, are most apparent. But focusing only on those areas of development can cause parents to miss many other important areas in which their children are growing and may need their help.

Although they may not occur simultaneously, the patterns of an adolescent's emotional growth mirror the patterns of her physical maturation. Neither progresses like a Sousa march, steadily and predictably moving from the beginning to end. Each is more like a piece of ragtime jazz, moving in complex fits and starts in what may appear to be several directions at once.

Teenagers' cognitive abilities—especially their skills at thinking abstractly and seeing a problem from several perspectives—improve considerably. They become increasingly concerned with abstract moral and ethical issues. Their perceptions of the world change from black-and-white to an overwhelming number of shades of gray. They can, often for the first time, see multiple solutions to problems and are no longer willing to accept their parents' rules and points of view without question.

Adolescents often show off their newfound skills by arguing—especially with their parents. Seldom are these arguments a rejection of the parent-child relationship. In fact they're quite the opposite, for they show how secure the teenager feels within the family. She knows that she can argue and makes mistakes, without risking that she'll no longer be accepted.

Friendships also change and take on a new importance. To younger children, friends are simply the people they do things with. The bond between them lies largely in their shared experiences. By late elementary school, however, children begin selecting friends at least in part because of their similar values and perceptions of the world. Friends and peers begin having a much stronger influence over how adolescents perceive themselves.

The latter years of adolescence also present predictable problems for families. Teenagers are trying to imagine what their impending separation from their parents will be like, and what it will mean for their relationships. They may awkwardly advance toward and then retreat from independence, apparently rejecting their parents one moment and clinging to them the next.

Some respond to the problem paradoxically. They're ashamed of how dependent they feel and of how afraid they are to separate from their parents. To handle these overwhelming feelings, they may get into loud and long arguments with their parents, seemingly trying to push them away as if they need to do that to complete their feared emotional separation.

Although parents worry that their children may suddenly and permanently develop fundamentally different values when they become teenagers, that seldom happens. While you can expect them to challenge many of your beliefs—and in fact you want them to do that—you should keep in mind that you've had a dozen or more years of near-total influence over your children. That influence almost always comes through on the important issues.

Rebels with a Cause

Although adolescence has long been portrayed as a necessarily stormy period that is fraught with emotional danger, child-development researchers generally agree that such descriptions are overblown. The vast majority of teenagers pass through adolescence with few or no psychological problems.

There will, of course, be some rough spots in this transition to adulthood. Here are some ideas to help you help your children during periods of emotional tension and confusion:

- Expect young teenagers to assert their need for independence in ways that may seem strange. It's not unusual for adolescents to go to the movies with their parents but to insist on sitting apart from them. A thirteen-year-old may ask you for a ride to a friend's house and insist that you drop him off a block or two away so that you won't be seen. (I'll discuss this further below.)

  There's nothing personal in these apparent rejections. They're simply awkward experiments with the autonomy of adulthood.

- Acknowledge your child's ambivalent feelings. Even contemplating moving away from home, starting college or a job, or leaving the known world of high school can be frightening to a teenager. Share some of your own memories of the concerns you had when you were that age. Let your child know that you're still supportive. That makes it safer for her to talk to you about these issues.

- Keep on talking to your children. Don't give up, even if your children seem not to be listening to you. They're actually paying closer attention than they're willing to admit. You need to have a heavy dose of patience and acceptance. Recognize that your children may be pushing you away for a while, but not forever. That separation may be necessary, but they'll come back.

Teenage Embarrassment

A child-development researcher I know once told me how, when he was thirteen years old and had just started junior high school, he began to loathe and fear one of his family's traditions: going to a particular restaurant for Sunday dinner. He worried that he might run into one of his classmates at the restaurant and his "cover would be blown."

After all, like his friends, he'd spent considerable time and effort at school trying to give the impression that he was mature, independent, and in charge of his own life. Being spotted with his parents would show them that the image he'd hoped to cultivate wasn't completely true. My friend admitted that it wasn't until he became an adult that it finally dawned on him that if his teenage friends had seen him at the restaurant, they'd be with *their* parents!

Embarrassment punctuates the relationship between young teenagers and their parents. Those feelings may be especially acute around the time of puberty, when adolescents develop strong conflicts over their growing need for autonomy and the recognition that they still are very much dependent upon the adults around them. The extent of their dependency becomes a secret that they try to hide from their peers, most of whom are vainly trying to do the same.[1]

Actually, children's feelings of embarrassment start well before adolescence. When and in which circumstances they occur

---

[1] Another psychologist friend of mine told me how, when her daughter was thirteen years old, she had asked the girl to accompany her on yet another errand. While they were in the car, her daughter turned to her and said through clenched teeth, "You know, this is the third time this week that I've gone somewhere with my *mother*!" My friend turned to her and, with all due seriousness, replied, "I won't tell a soul." Her daughter thanked her and breathed a sigh of relief.

reflect the combination of children's growing intellectual abilities and social awareness. Eighteen-month-olds will sometimes show awkwardness and shyness when people pay attention to them. They need not be misbehaving. In fact, they may become embarrassed when they receive compliments. This shows that they are aware of themselves as individuals.

By the time they're two or three years old, they show a different and more sophisticated form of embarrassment that involves feelings of shame or a recognition that something they have done is inappropriate. This type of embarrassment reflects their growing social sense, for this is also the age at which they first show pride in themselves.

But it isn't until early adolescence that they are likely to have feelings of embarrassment that have to do with their parents. This is a time when they're not only struggling with their increased need for autonomy, but they're becoming acutely aware of social pressure.

No longer do adolescents view their parents as the omniscient, godlike creatures they appeared to be only a few years earlier. Now their parents' flaws—both real and imagined—stand out sharply. They respond by trying to distance themselves from the imperfections.

While parents often find this change in their children's behavior desconcerting, you can take solace in the fact that this intense stage of embarrassment lasts for just a few years. By the nineth or tenth grade, most teenagers are proud to be seen with their parents again.

Handling Embarrassing Feelings

Not only is it normal for teenagers to feel embarrassed by their parents, but it can be a good sign as well. Children who are the most socially in tune with their peers are the ones who are the most likely to be embarrassed by their parents. Children who are perceived as socially awkward or "nerds" are less likely to be embarrassed by their parents, because they identify more closely with adults than with their peers.

Here are some other things you should keep in mind if your teenager suddenly (or routinely) finds you embarrassing:

- Pick your battles carefully. You don't really lose anything (except perhaps a bit of pride) if your children ask you to drop them off a block from their friend's house so that you remain out of sight. But if your children insist that you leave the house while they throw a party, you should refuse to do so. This is a matter of safety and responsibility, not social propriety.

- Look for new approaches that encourage autonomy. Adolescents will find going to the movies with their families more tolerable if their parents give them money for tickets and popcorn ahead of time. This recognizes their need to be different from the younger children who are attending the movie and gives them more of the symbolic control that they crave. It may also help to let them invite friends, since that changes the tenor of the evening.

- Never retaliate against an adolescent by publicly embarrassing the child further or by saying that he or she embarrasses you. That's likely to be crushing to a teenager. Remember that the emotional pain of embarrassment is far more acute during adolescence than at any other stage of life. Not only are children this age extremely sensitive, but they're convinced that their behavior and appearance is the focus of everyone's attention.

Depression in Adolescence

Dr. Barry Garfinkel, the former chief of child psychiatry at the University of Minnesota, has an interesting way of categorizing the symptoms of the emotional problems in the children he treats. He refers to them as "onion symptoms" and "garlic symptoms." Onion symptoms are behaviors that irritate other people. Garlic symptoms are things that bother the child, giving him, in effect, a case of emotional heartburn.

Parents routinely spot the onion symptoms in their children—things like aggression or temper tantrums. They have much more difficulty seeing the garlic symptoms, such as anxiety, withdrawal, and depression.

The most commonly overlooked problem—and the most commonly missed diagnosis by professionals as well—is depression.

It is especially tragic in those relatively few instances in which it leads to suicide, for it represents the antithesis of all that we wish childhood to be. Depression is anger and frustration that the child turns against himself. While a certain amount of depression is a normal part of growing up, the limited skills that children have for coping with stress can make their depressions acutely painful and confusing.

Unlike depressed adults, who from the first are likely to tell someone they feel sad, depressed children may mask the obvious symptoms of their problem with behavior that, to many parents and teachers, appears to contradict the diagnosis. Many teenagers who get into trouble at school or with the law are actually depressed. So are some children who appear hostile and aggressive. While the behavior problems are noticed by adults, the inner turmoil is missed.

The most common signs of depression in an adolescent often include a general slowing down of his physical activity and a growing isolation from friends. A depressed teenager may watch two or three hours of television after coming home from school and then go up to his room and listen to music for a few hours.

Like depressed adults, teenagers may show marked changes in their sleep patterns: difficulty falling asleep, waking up early, or sleeping many more hours than usual. They may talk about feeling worthless and hopeless. Girls, more than boys, are likely to overeat.

There may be less obvious signs of a problem with depression, including behavior that, at first blush, appears to be mature and constructive. For example, some teenagers whose grades at school are dropping and who feel alienated will throw themselves into their schoolwork. Such atypical dedication may be a sign that the child is feeling hopeless about his situation.

The most serious consequence of depression is suicide. Although only a small percentage of depressed adolescents commit suicide, a very large proportion of teenagers who kill themselves are depressed at the time. Suicide is currently the second leading cause of death in America for people between the ages of fifteen and twenty-four. Over the past thirty years the suicide rate for this group has nearly tripled. Teenagers are especially at risk for suicide if they're both depressed and abusing alcohol. Any child who fits that pattern should be referred for help immediately.

If Your Teenager Seems Depressed

Everyone gets the blues at times. But clinical depression is very different from simply feeling emotionally low. It's a disease that requires treatment.

Few parents would hesitate to have their child evaluated and treated by a specialist if they suspected he suffered from, say, diabetes. Yet many parents and teachers are confused about and reluctant to seek help for a child who's seriously depressed. They worry about the social stigma of labeling a teenager as having an emotional problem.[2] They believe that, with time, the child will "snap out of it."

Here are some rules of thumb for deciding whether you should have your child evaluated by a child psychologist or psychiatrist:

---

[2] I've grown increasingly uncomfortable with the phrase *emotional problem* to describe depression since there's considerable and growing evidence that there's a clear biochemical basis for the symptoms. It's no less a disease than diabetes or anemia.

- Is the depression interfering with his performance at school? If a teacher calls to express concern about a significant change in your child's school work or socializing, or if you notice such changes yourself, you should consider having your child evaluated.

- If your child appears depressed for the first time and the condition lasts more than two weeks, he may need treatment. If the symptoms are mild and go away by themselves in a week or so, you probably shouldn't be concerned.

- If the problem has occurred before, you should pay closer attention to it, even if it doesn't last very long. The pattern of recurrence may point to a biological cause for the depression. In many cases, psychotherapy may help teach your child coping skills so that next time he can deal better with the situations that trigger or exacerbate his symptoms.

Leaving Home

All children (we hope) eventually leave home. For most, this separation comes at a predictable and ritualized period of their lives, such as the start of college or the beginning of a marriage. For others, especially young teenagers, moving out of their home can be an attempt to protect themselves, an act of rebellion, or a cry for help.

It's important to distinguish between two types of premature departures: moving toward another support system, and simply running away from home with an eye toward escape. The former can be a very positive experience for an adolescent; the latter is much more likely to be terrifying and self-destructive. I'll look at constructive ways that teenagers can spend time away from their parents in this section, and at the issues involved in potentially destructive acts, such as running away from home, in the next section.

When a colleague of mine, who's now a professor of child development, was fifteen years old, he told his parents that he couldn't live with them anymore. He moved in with his grandmother, who lived in another neighborhood in Brooklyn, New York. The adults stayed in close touch, relaying information about what my friend was doing. Three weeks later, tired of the long commute to his high school and in need of some fresh clothes, my friend returned home.

His adventure of moving to his grandmother's apartment was simply a break he needed from the pressures of his family life. In retrospect, he sees that experience, as well as the other times he spent away from his parents during various summers, as important steps toward maturity.[3]

It's common for adolescents to look for ways to explore who they are and to see how they fit into the world. The timing may reflect biological changes in their brains, for they can now think differently than they did only a year or two earlier. They can readily imagine new solutions to problems or different approaches to situations. Their world is no longer black-and-white, but a complex mosaic of grays. An explosion in the possibilities

---

[3] He recently was on the receiving end of a similar situation when his wife's fourteen-year-old niece lived with them for several weeks to see what life was like outside of the town in which she lived.

they can envision for their lives calls them to reexamine their sense of identity and whom they might become. They can picture themselves, often for the first time, as independent from their parents.

For many, spending time away from their immediate families is a normal and appropriate way of testing their new ways of thinking and of forming relationships. These children are very different from runaways, whose dramatic actions often point to serious underlying emotional problems for them or their families.

One way of differentiating the two is to ask yourself why the adolescent is leaving home. Is he running away from issues such as how he should deal with authority, or is this a mature decision to move out because he needs a different environment at that moment in order to grow emotionally?

These excursions are psychological as well as physical, whether they take place in a structured summer program or through an informal stay with a relative or a friend's parents. They allow the teenager to shed the mantle of the past and to try on new roles and styles of relationships.

It also helps to have a historical perspective on this. Although today's families assume it to be normal, the idea of children living with their parents until they are eighteen is quite new. As recently as a century ago, when few teenagers attended high school, adolescents from all social classes were routinely placed with family members or even strangers when they reached puberty. Earlier generations did it at even younger ages. In the seventeenth century, children were often sent to learn a trade and live in other people's homes when they were about ten or eleven.

In those days, the reasons for leaving one's parents were more likely to be economic than psychological. For most families, adolescence was a time for work. Even those teenagers who went to school usually lived far from home.

Deciding to Move Out

Try not to overreact if your teenager says that he wants to live somewhere else. Listen to your child before you speak. Keep in mind that your goals are to understand the reasons behind your child's request and to find safe and appropriate ways to meet his needs. Here are some specific suggestions:

- Remember that children at different stages of adolescence have different emotional needs. Sometimes those needs can be met without the child's spending time away from home. For example, twelve- and thirteen-year-olds are usually struggling with issues of control over their own lives. They're more interested in being able to exercise that control by making decisions than in what or how important those decisions are.

  For example, a twelve-year-old who announces that he can't stand living at home may be upset over the fact that his bedtime hasn't changed in two years, or that his parents insist that he start his homework as soon as he comes home from school. By letting him negotiate a new bedtime or giving him more control of his schedule (within reason, of course), you may be able to defuse the situation quickly.

Children in late adolescence (roughly ages sixteen to eighteen) are more interested in the types of decisions they're allowed to make. They're concerned about their future, not just rebelling against their parents.

A sixteen-year-old might need a safe way of testing what it would be like to live away from home, if only for a few days or weeks. He won't express that need in those words, of course. By recognizing that need, you can help your child test his independence in safe and appropriate ways.

- Help your child plan his time away from home. This gives him the message that you have faith in his maturity—something most adolescents are desperate to hear. It also helps you ensure that his plans are reasonable and safe.

  Explore alternatives, such as spending some time with a relative or taking part in a supervised summer work project. Discuss other options, such as spending several weekends away instead of the same number of days in a row.

- Stay in close touch with the people your child will stay with. Explain any special concerns you may have. If the stay is for more than a few days, agree on ways to communicate regularly with both those adults and your child.

- Let go. Remember that the more resistant you are to your child's emotional growth, the more of a struggle it will become. Some parents have a very difficult time giving their adolescents enough opportunities to make their own decisions. Being too restrictive can provoke the rebellious and possibly dangerous behavior you're trying to avoid.

Runaways

The literature of youth is filled with romantic portrayals of children who run or live away from home. Huck Finn sets off for adventure on his raft. Pippi Longstocking travels happily with her animal friends. What child could pass up such wonderful opportunities?

The realities of life on the street are not the least bit romantic. But to a teenager who feels trapped and rejected, running away may feel like the only option.

The U.S. Department of Health and Human Services estimates that up to 1.5 million American children run away from home each year. About 200,000 are on the streets at any one time. Most are sixteen years old.

Studies of teenage runaways show that about half return home within twenty-four hours. The majority of the remainder come back within two or three days. Only a small proportion stay away longer, and these are in the most danger.

Threatening to run away is often a call for help. It's a way of expressing a problem that the child is having trouble talking about directly. Preadolescents and adolescents are less reliant on their parents than younger children for their basic needs. Their threats to leave home can be carried out more easily. Even when they don't leave, children who make threats are giving you important information about how they feel and the limited options they see. Their threats can serve as a springboard for discussing those emotions and searching for additional options.

Among those teenagers who run away repeatedly, a significant proportion appear to be trying to escape some sort of abuse by adults. Research by Dr. Mark-David Janus, a Paulist priest and a clinical psychologist at Indiana University Medical School, has found that 73 percent of chronic runaways said they had been physically beaten and 51 percent said they had been sexually abused. (Because these were children who had run away several times and who had sought help at a children's shelter, those percentages are higher than they would be for the general population of runaways.)

More common for first-time runaways and those who threaten to leave are feelings that they are no longer respected or even wanted. They feel their parents are unwilling to listen to them and to acknowledge how they are changing. Running away is, in their eyes, a way to simultaneously show their independence and regain their parents' attention.

Many of these children see their parents as having high expectations for them and very rigid rules, but not giving them the emotional support they need. What parents intend as protective acts, such as setting rules about how late their children can stay out, these adolescents interpret as rejection.

Remember that if they could see an alternative, these children wouldn't want to leave home. They want their relationship with their parents to be different. Running away is an impulsive, emotional solution to their problem of not seeing any other way to change the ways they relate to their parents.

Dealing with the Threat to Run Away

Most of the times children threaten to run away occur in the middle of an argument with their parents. It's a time when neither side is likely to be thinking clearly or looking beyond the moment. If your child does say she wants to leave, here are some ways to analyze and approach the problem:

- Take seriously—but not literally—what your child says. Almost all children will talk about running away at some point. Sometimes young children will use such a threat to express anger at you or as a way of testing whether you love them.

  Let your child know that you can see she's very upset. Tell her that you love her even when she gets angry or sad. Simply acknowledging her feelings will often allow her to talk about the underlying problem.

- Recognize that a threat to run away is a sign of a communication problem at the very least. Help your child articulate her complaints. Listen without cutting her off. If you approach your conversation honestly and with good intentions, that will encourage your child to take the same approach.

- Never dare your child to make good on her threat. Remember that running away from home is usually an impulsive act. Don't tease her by packing her bags or telling her to leave. That's humiliating and scary.

  With a preteen or a younger child, you can say something like, "Listen, I'm not going to let you run away. It's not safe." That simple statement usually answers her unasked questions about whether you love and value her.

  With an older child, you should take a slightly different approach. Begin by stating that you want her to live at home. Give your reasons for wanting that. Let her know that if she leaves home, you're going to look for her. Then you can talk about the things that are bothering her, and look for ways to address them. Those opening statements give an adolescent the recognition she craves of her improved ability to think and solve problems, and reassures her that you care about what happens to her.

- Don't feel you have to handle the problem yourself. It's often helpful to have an experienced psychotherapist or counselor act as an intermediary. It's much easier for a teenager to hear criticism from an outside adult. That therapist also becomes an advocate for the child in setting appropriate family rules that recognize both his growth and his limitations.

- Look for a safety valve. Sometimes children (and their parents as well) need a cooling-off period. If a child is threatening to run away, consider arranging a place for her to run to, where she can be with a surrogate parent, such as an aunt or grandparent. Don't simply let her run off to be with a friend; that suggests that you feel she no longer needs the support and protection of adults. If you work with your child on planning some time apart, she's less likely to see your actions as a rejection than if you simply send her away.

The Driver's License

It may seem strange at first to have a section on driving in this chapter. I've found, however, that falling in love for the first time and obtaining a driver's license are perhaps the two most profound events in an adolescent's emotional development. Both are watersheds in how teenagers perceive themselves. I'll deal with love and dating in Chapter 5.

To most American teenagers, the symbolic value of a driver's license goes far beyond the legal right to drive. It is a token of their power and independence, an opportunity for privacy and romance, and a sign of increased status that can separate them from younger friends and siblings.

For many, a driver's license is their clearest rite of passage into adulthood. While teenagers at school or on the job are treated differently from adults, behind the wheel they have the same rights, responsibilities, and benefits as someone twice their age.

A friend of mine, who now teaches developmental psychology, recalled how he was so excited when his learner's permit arrived in the mail that he insisted his mother immediately let him get behind the wheel of the family car. She reluctantly agreed and, after climbing into the passenger seat, began showing him what to do.

My friend, with all the righteous indignation a teenager could muster, looked at his mother and said, "Mom, I know how to drive!" He then floored the accelerator with the car in reverse, and lunged backward into a busy street. His mother screamed for him to hit the brakes. When they finally stopped, she took away the keys and told him that his father would be the one to teach him to drive.

Although teenagers are, with few exceptions, enthusiastic about driving, parents often have mixed feelings. Many of the parents' concerns are pragmatic. In the United States, nearly four out of every five deaths of teenagers between the ages of fifteen and nineteen are due to accidents. The majority of those accidents involve motor vehicles, a statistic that is reflected in the disproportionately high insurance premiums paid by teenage drivers and their families.[4]

Those figures point to the psychological and developmental factors that separate teenagers from adults. Although their reflexes and physical coordination are at their peak, the psychological makeup of adolescents is, in many cases, antithetical to safe driving. A child psychiatrist I know phrases it this way: "Driving is like sex. Physical ability precedes emotional capability."

Teenagers tend to feel invulnerable. They have not yet shed

---

[4] As I write this, the seventeen-year-old son of a friend of ours has joined our family. I discovered that adding him to our automobile insurance policy after he gets his license will more than double our payments.

the idea that accidents only happen to other people. They often have difficulties understanding the consequences of their actions. Paradoxically, they often have a strong sense of inadequacy that goes along with their feelings of invulnerability. The driver's license can help them prove, in their own minds, that they have status and power. That can make them very dangerous when they're behind the wheel.

That danger is greater at night than during the day. According to research published in the *Journal of the American Medical Association*, although teenagers do only about 20 percent of their driving at night, more than 50 percent of their fatal car accidents occur at this time. Also, even though they are less likely than older drivers to drive after drinking, those teenagers who do so are at a higher risk of being in a crash than adults, even though they have drunk less alcohol than adults. Reduced visibility, combined with alcohol, appears to make night driving especially dangerous for the inexperienced.

Not all teenagers are bad drivers or risk takers, of course. Much of their day-to-day behavior will give their parents clear indications of what they will be like as drivers. How do they deal with frustration? Are they able to plan ahead? How have they handled their personal finances? Do they use seat belts as passengers? What is their attitude toward breaking the law, especially in the areas of alcohol and drug abuse?

Teenagers drive as they live. If they're mature in other ways, they'll usually act maturely when they're on the road. Research on teenage drivers has shown that the old stereotype of the Milquetoast becoming aggressive when behind the wheel just isn't true.

While most adolescents who want a driver's license take some sort of formal driver-education course, most of their driver education comes from watching how their parents drive and learning how they take risks and treat other drivers and the law. Also, you can't rely on a training course to turn your teenager into a safe driver. The Insurance Institute for Highway Safety has found evidence that driver-education programs in schools may lead to a net increase in car accidents by encouraging students to obtain licenses at a younger age.[5]

Also, there can be a big difference between when the law says a child is entitled to drive and when parents feel their own child has the skills and attitude to do so safely. It's important that parents exercise their power and responsibility. If they don't feel their child is emotionally ready to drive, they should refuse to let him get a learner's permit. If their child is acting dangerously, they should take the permit away. For many sixteen-year-olds, however, the prospect of getting a learner's permit is such a powerful incentive that parents can use it as an effective tool in persuading them to change some old and bothersome habits.

One way to handle your concerns about your child's driving after he gets his license is to monitor his behavior closely for several months or even longer as he drives in increasingly stressful and difficult situations.[6] For example, in the beginning you might only allow your child to drive if a parent is in the passenger seat. Develop a list of safe driving behaviors together. Make sure, for example, that he's using his seatbelt and signaling his turns 100 percent of the time, not just most of the time. Only permit

---

[5] Connecticut, which eliminated high school driver education, has seen its teenage accident rate go down as the average age of new drivers has risen.

[6] Many teenagers will, of course, resist this with great vigor. Just keep in mind that you still own the car and that driving is a privilege, not a right. Besides, an unwillingness to cooperate on this matter is a good sign that the child isn't emotionally ready to drive.

daytime and local driving for the first few months.[7] As you grow more confident of his abilities and maturity, expand his privileges.

Rules of the Road

If your child, like most, gets a driver's license before leaving high school, there are some things you can do to increase his safety behind the wheel:

- Set clear ground rules ahead of time, whether your child is using the family car or his own. Will he have any additional responsibilities around the house in exchange for the new privileges? Will he pay for his own gas and a percentage of repair bills and insurance premiums? Reinforce the idea that driving is a privilege, not a right. Set clear rules and consequences for drinking, drug use, and other reckless and dangerous behavior.

- Let your child comment on your driving. Those comments should be both positive and negative. It's easier and emotionally less threatening for an adolescent to learn about safe driving by studying how someone else drives. Ask your child to point out the times when you don't use a turn signal or fail to come to a complete stop or appropriately adjust

---

[7] Some governments are institutionalizing this approach. New York State doesn't allow teenagers to drive late at night. New Zealand issues restricted licenses for the first eighteen months that not only limit driving hours but also prohibit carrying passengers unless an adult is in the car.

your speed because of bad weather. Remember that you can't expect your children to listen to you unless you've listened to them.

- Focus on specific behaviors, not personality traits. Comments like "You're too close to the car ahead of you" or "You did a good job of checking for traffic" are much more useful than "You're a reckless driver." That way you're both clear on what exactly should be changed and what the driver is doing well.

- Give your child lots of practice with you in the car, especially after your child gets his license. Supervised practice can help your child build his driving skills more quickly than unsupervised time in the driver's seat.

4

Friends and Peer Pressure

Friendship is a common belief in the same fallacies, mountebanks and hobgoblins.

—H. L. MENCKEN (1880–1956)

It is the theme of numerous Hollywood movies: a teenager led astray, at least temporarily, by spending time with a "bad influence." Although many parents feel such fears deeply, the reality of those relationships is usually quite different, according to psychologists who study children's friendships. Most of those potentially harmful peer relationships are short-lived and may actually serve a useful purpose for both children. (That really would, of course, be less interesting as a film plot.)

Parents often think peer influence is more powerful than the research shows it to be. They overlook the fact that teenagers generally pick friends on the basis of shared interests and attitudes. Not all friends fit that mold, of course. This is especially true during early adolescence, when children are struggling awkwardly with ways to assert their independence from their families.

At the same time, however, young adolescents crave member-ship in a group. That's one reason they may rail against their parents' conformity while simultaneously dressing, acting, and speaking in ways that are identical to those of their peers.[1] Wearing a nose ring or shaving half your head is a much safer act of rebellion if other people in your school or neighborhood are doing it as well.

Research has shown that peer relationships are much more influential on superficial areas, such as what clothes and music children like and how they should behave in certain situations. They aren't as influential on moral views, educational and career goals, and religious values, which are much more affected by parents than by friends.

Befriending someone who is, from the parents' perspective, potentially a bad influence is one way a teenager can experiment with a different lifestyle. It works the other way as well, of course. While a cautious, academically successful girl may be examining a different approach to life by spending time with a schoolmate who boasts of her ability to shoplift, the second girl may be using the friendship to discover what it feels like to be successful in other areas.

By spending time with an avid skateboarder, artist, athlete, or even a petty thief, a teenager can live some aspect of that person's life vicariously and see how well it fits in with her own beliefs. While some adolescents use these friendships as gateways into new lifestyles, most are simply testing their parents' and their own values in a relatively risk-free way.

---

[1] Although it's a bit simplistic, this is also a large reason why many young adolescents who feel alienated, hopeless, and angry find joining a youth gang so appealing. It gives them a sense of belonging, as well as the illusion of power, purpose, and importance.

This type of experimentation with friendships is also a reflection of how your child has matured. Before they become teenagers, children tend to see friendships as an all-or-nothing proposition. Adolescents, however, can now see their friends' positive and negative attributes. A fourteen-year-old can describe a friend as someone she might want to spend a Saturday evening socializing with, but not someone she'd want to study for a math test with.

Friendships that lead an adolescent to engage in very risky behavior, however, are a different matter. A relationship that threatens a child's health or welfare, perhaps because it involves using drugs or engaging in unsafe or premature sex, calls for immediate action from parents.

One way to tell whether there's a potentially serious problem with a friendship is to look for changes in a child's behavior when she's not with her new friend. While many adolescents may appear moody or uncommunicative at times, teenagers who are in destructive relationships often show these problems acutely. They may stop bringing friends home, or become secretive about where and with whom they're spending their time. They may become withdrawn or secretive, have difficulty sleeping, and have a striking drop in their grades at school.[2]

Unfortunately, some of the things parents do in response to their children's questionable friendships can inadvertently make matters worse. Simply prohibiting your child from associating with this new friend is likely to backfire. The more you tell a teenager not to be with a particular person, the more attractive

---

[2] This pattern of behavior may also reflect an underlying clinical depression, which is a significant but often-overlooked problem for adolescents. If untreated, it puts them at risk for serious problems, including suicide.

that person becomes. (Psychologists sometimes refer to this as the Romeo and Juliet effect.) In fact, children who hear their friends being critized by parents are likely to rush to their friends' defense, even if the connection between them isn't strong.

A better approach would be to look at what each child is getting out of the relationship. By talking to your own child about this, you can help her analyze what she likes and dislikes about her friend. How does she feel about herself when she's with this friend as compared with her other friends? Encourage her to talk about what she feels makes a good friendship, so that she can reach her own conclusions about how this particular friend fills that role.

Understanding Friendships

Films such as *Heathers, Dead Poets Society, Boyz N the Hood, The Breakfast Club,* and *Some Kind of Wonderful*—all of which are available on videotape—can be excellent jumping-off points for talking with teenagers about inappropriate friendships and the power of peer influence. Help your children explore the social pressures the characters feel, and discuss how the choices they make affect their lives.

Here are some other things to keep in mind when talking to your teenage children about friendships that might lead to problems:

- Set limits on behavior, not on people. If you tell your child not to hang out with someone, you're fighting a losing battle. Instead, talk about the specific behaviors you don't want her to do, such as going to an unsupervised party or hanging around the local shopping mall.

- Focus any criticism you may have of your child's friends on their behaviors, not on their appearance or personality. Comments about hairstyle, clothing, or choices in music are likely to make your child leap to her friend's defense. Instead, try to see the friend from your child's perspective.

  One way to do this is to make your house the kind of place that your child feels comfortable bringing friends to. This has much more to do with attitude than with furnishings. Those visits will help you get to know your child's friends and to make more informed and intelligent judgments about them.

- Temper any negative comments about your child's friends with positive ones. ("I like John's passion and enthusiasm for music. It shows how creative he can be. But I wish he would act more respectfully toward us when he comes to visit. What would be a good way to let him know that he should thank us when we feed him dinner or a snack?") That allows your child to think about the real issue without becoming defensive about her friend.

- Respect your teenager's improved ability to think. Nothing will alienate an adolescent faster than the feeling that you're talking down to her. Teenagers are rightfully proud of their newfound abilities to think about complex social and personal problems. Make clear what your attitudes and standards for behavior are, but listen to what she has to say as well so that she doesn't feel like you're treating her the way you did when she was younger.

Despite their improved ability to reason, adolescents still have difficulty envisioning future consequences of their current behavior. It's better to focus on the immediate outcomes of your child's problem behavior, such as feeling embarrassed in front of friends, than on the possible long-term consequences, like not getting into college.

- Discuss other ways your child can experience new things and meet new friends. Look for safe ways your child can experiment with different lifestyles. Some of the best after-school programs, such as sports teams and drama groups, help adolescents bolster their self-esteem through organized and adult-supervised activities.

Resisting Social Pressure

I used to have a sign in my office that mocked the simplistic and ineffective government-sanctioned approach of the 1980s to teaching children how to resist involvement in drugs and sex. The sign read, *"Just say no!" has done for drug abusers what "Have a nice day!" has done for chronic depressives.*

There's good reason for my cynicism about the Reagan-era dictum, just as there's good reason to take very seriously the issues those approaches tried to take on. One of the most difficult tasks of childhood is learning how to resist social pressure. The challenges to teenagers come from many directions: a dare to shoplift an article of clothing, an invitation to use an illegal drug, a demand for sexual intimacy, an offer to join a gang.

Resisting such pressure is more complex than it appears. It requires that adolescents think about the possible consequences of their behavior and that they feel emotionally strong enough to risk rejection by a peer or friend. It also requires a sense of empathy for the person applying the pressure, and the ability and self-confidence to propose different behaviors.

Researchers who have studied how children respond to social pressures of all types have found that some are more likely than others to cave in. At particular risk are children who feel few emotional ties to their families. If a child is lonely and isolated, and a group comes along that offers membership and a sense of affiliation, the child may welcome that, even if the group is a gang or a cult.

An adolescent whose parents are domineering is also at risk for being manipulated, even though the parents often think their behavior inoculates the child against getting into trouble. This is a case of a certain amount of rebellion being a good thing. Children who feel intimidated by their parents and unwilling to question them are more likely to take the same approach when faced by a seemingly powerful peer. But if the child has had practice in making his own decisions and anticipating their consequences, then he's better prepared to do the same thing when he's told by a peer to do something potentially dangerous.

Learning how to respond to social pressure is a skill that is separate from moral values and personal philosophies. Like other skills, it's sharpened more through coaching and practice than through dogma. Simply telling a teenager "Just say no!" or explaining the reasons why he shouldn't do something doesn't go far enough.[3]

Such simplistic approaches ignore the social pressure felt by teenagers and younger children, and do not give them a way of maintaining social relationships while refusing to give in. A child who can respond to a friend's invitation to get drunk with a simple counteroffer to go to a movie is more likely not only to avoid problems with alcohol but also to maintain the friendship. Simply saying no is seldom enough to get a child out of this type of situation, especially if the social pressure is coming from a friend or someone your child would like to have as a friend.

Teaching Decision Making

A good first step toward helping your teenager resist social pressure is to talk about some of the decisions you made as an adolescent, and to share some of the ones you're making as an adult. Instead of doing this as a one-shot formal lecture—something many teenagers will resist—weave these discussions into your daily conversations.

Think through some of your current decisions out loud,

---

[3] Another significant problem with approaches such as "Just say no!" is that they imply that someone who says yes even once is a bad person. Teenagers need to feel that just because they tried a drug or a sexual activity once doesn't mean they can't say no the next time. There's evidence that a significant number of adolescents who try certain illegal drugs stop after one or two experiences.

evaluating the short-term and long-term pros and cons. Help your child see how you weigh the alternatives.

Here are some other ideas to consider:

- Give children practice in making decisions. With young children this can be as simple as choosing which cereal to eat for breakfast, what clothes to wear, and which baseball cards to trade. For teenagers, the decisions should be both more complex and more important. Remember that the process of making a decision and being responsible for its outcome is much more important than the choice itself.

- When you talk to your children about how they make specific, ordinary decisions, don't turn the conversation into an inquisition or criticism, especially if you disagree with their choices. That will cause them to stop listening. Remember that your goal is to help your children get better at thinking through alternatives.

- Do some role-playing with a group of children and perhaps their parents. Act out some skits with your children that involve real-life situations in which they have to make a choice.[4] What should you do if someone dares you to ride on the back bumper of a bus? What if you haven't finished your homework

---

[4] Although younger teenagers sometimes feel comfortable doing this at home, older teens often prefer to try role-playing at school or in an after-school group, and with adults other than their parents.

and someone you really like asks you to go to the movies? What if someone offers you a drink or some drugs at a party? Does it matter if it's a stranger or a friend? What if a boy says he'll spread rumors about you at school if you don't have sex with him?

Have the children try solving these problems in different ways to see what the responses might be. Then they can talk about whether their responses sounded phony or effective.

- Expect children to make some bad decisions. That is, after all, why you're trying to give them lots of practice—especially in situations that don't have severe or long-term negative consequences. Sometimes they can learn more by recovering from their mistakes than by making the right decision the first time.

Popularity

When a friend of mine was thirteen years old, he felt cursed by his twenty-twenty vision. It seemed that all the popular kids in his class wore glasses. To fit in better with that popular crowd, he pretended to be having trouble reading. Even though his parents knew that their son's vision was good, they arranged for his eye doctor to give him glasses with nonrefracting lenses so that he could feel better about himself.

Another friend, who attended junior high school in Brooklyn

in the late 1950s, told me that he soon discovered that the height of fashion was to wear pants with a buckle in the back. The buckles were ugly and uncomfortable when he sat down, but those were small prices to pay for social acceptance. He even remembers wanting to paint a picture of a buckle on one of his less fashionable pairs of pants so that he'd fit in.

My friends' seventh-grade worries about being popular were and continue to be typical. Children begin talking about popularity from their earliest school experiences. They watch the most popular children to find out whether they should wear expensive but loosely tied athletic shoes and brightly colored baggy shorts this year, or whether those styles are passé.[5] They listen for what special words they should be using to show that they are up-to-date.

Parents also worry that their children may not be popular enough. We may imagine dire consequences if they are not in the "in" group. Yet psychologists who study popularity and how it differs from friendship say that most of the time popularity has little effect on a child's development. Simply having one or more friends is much more important.

One way researchers begin studying patterns of friendships at school is by asking children to write down who their closest friends are, and seeing whether those claims of friendship are reciprocated, at least on paper. They measure popularity, however, by asking children to write down the names of two or three classmates they like the most and those they like the least. Usually

---

[5] These styles can actually tell you a lot about your child's emotional development. In the early 1990s one of the "in" styles for teenage girls was to wear tight pants and oversized tops. This was probably in part a reflection of their ambivalent feelings about their sexuality.

a small cluster of children get the most votes on either end, showing them to be the most popular or the most rejected. The majority of children fall somewhere in the middle.

The children rated as most popular tend to have stable characteristics that can be seen as early as preschool. These include having a sense of humor, having good social skills, and being fun to be around. Adhering to traditional sex roles, being physically attractive, and being intelligent also seem to help a child become popular.

Despite the assumptions of many parents and children, studies show few long-term differences between the most popular children and the ones in the middle group. The children psychologists worry about the most are the ones who are consistently rejected. Not being among the most popular is not, by itself, a problem or a predictor of future problems.

Although many of the rejected children are treated that way because they're bullies or they lack social skills, other are rejected simply because they don't seem to fit in. They may wear the "wrong" clothes or look different in some other way. Weight seems to be important, too, especially if the child has been overweight for a few years.

Being rejected by classmates for several years as a child has implications for adulthood as well. Socially rejected children have a high probability of getting into trouble as adults.

Rejections can be a particular problem for children who have just started attending a new school, especially if they are young adolescents who didn't make the transition with friends from their old school. They may feel lost, not only in the new buildings but in their new social groups. These children's heartfelt pleas for a particular article of clothing or hairstyle—even if it seems out of character—may be more than a simple submission to peer pressure. It may be a way of avoiding rejection and the problems that come with it.

Helping Your Child Be Liked

Although forming and maintaining friendships is fundamentally your child's responsibility, there are some things you can do to help if your child is having difficulty or is being socially rejected. Here are some ideas:

- If your child says, "Nobody likes me," do not immediately disagree. It's tempting to correct your child when you know such a statement is not true. But if you disagree quickly, your child will feel like even more of an outcast and will keep his feelings to himself.

    Instead, ask your child why he feels that he's disliked. Encourage him to keep talking, both to explain the situation and to ventilate his feelings. Ask what he (or the two of you) might be able to do to change the situation.

- Listen closely to your child's suggestions. Seemingly silly things, such as cutting strategically placed holes in a pair of inexpensive pants, can make a young adolescent feel much more a part of a social group. Buying a new outfit or switching from eyeglasses to contact lenses can be a worthwhile investment—

although it won't make much of a difference if social skills are the underlying problem.

- Don't worry about your teenager's experimentation with such things as hairstyle and clothing. Remember that it's important for adolescents to test ways they can be different from adults yet similar to their peers. Fashion is a relatively safe way of rebelling. Besides, in a few years your child's lime-green baggy shorts will probably suffer the same fate as your old Nehru jacket or vinyl go-go boots.

- Get your child involved in outside groups such as YMCAs, Girls Inc., and weekend sports programs that draw children from other schools. Meeting new teenagers can help break a cycle of rejection. Sometimes a child just needs a better match so that he gets practice making friends. Those skills and that confidence can transfer to school.

Shyness

It can be painful to watch very shy children: They are often overwhelmed and tense, acutely aware of their vulnerabilities. For many young children, timidity around new people is a temporary response to stress at home. For a few, it's a part of a larger set of anxieties and discomforts that last through adolescence and into adulthood.

Shyness is remarkably common. According to research by Dr. Philip Zimbardo of Stanford University, it reaches a peak in early adolescence. About 50 percent of boys and 60 percent of girls in American junior high schools say that they feel shy. By the time they're ages eighteen to twenty-one, that number drops to 44 percent.[6]

Although most people equate shyness with timidity or awkwardness in social situations, especially with unfamiliar people, psychologists who study it say shyness is more complex. Shy people show characteristic patterns in their thoughts, emotions, and physiology.

A shy student faced with making a presentation or even asking a question in a classroom will probably judge herself and her abilities harshly and negatively. She will be very anxious, and show that anxiety through physical symptoms such as a racing heart, sweaty palms, or blushing. But looking only at timid behavior can be misleading. Shy people have negative thoughts and anxiety along with the physiological changes. They're comfortable only when they're playing a highly structured role.[7]

Teachers sometimes misinterpret shy children's behavior as boredom or disinterest, and tend to overlook those children when asked to identify the brightest ones in the class. Persistent shyness in adulthood often leads to significant problems. According to research by Dr. Jonathan Cheek at Wellesley College, acutely shy adults tend to make less money, are underemployed, don't get

---

[6] Dr. Zimbardo also surveyed college students in other countries about shyness. The lowest rate of self-reported shyness was in Israel, with 31 percent. The highest was Japan (57 percent) and Taiwan (55 percent).

[7] In fact, Dr. Zimbardo has found that many stand-up comedians, talk show hosts, actors, and politicians are shy.

promoted, and stay in unsatisfactory jobs. They tend to be lonely, to get married at a later age if at all, not to have as many friends, and to be dissatisfied with their friendships.

For a few shy children, however, social withdrawal can be advantageous if they find rewarding and nonthreatening ways to spend their time. If such temperamentally shy children are intelligent and do well in school, and have parents who value academic success, those are the children who often end up as valedictorians.

Helping a Child Gain Confidence

Probably the worst thing you can do to a shy teenager is to tease her about being shy. That will simply escalate her anxieties and increase her shyness. The best approaches involve nudging rather than pushing.

Here are some other things to keep in mind, especially for children in their early teens and younger:

- Don't pin negative labels on your child. Hearing her parents call her "dumb" or "fat" will contribute to a child's low self-esteem and social anxiety. Also, don't call your child "shy." Parents often use that label when they're feeling uncomfortable with their child's behavior. That teaches the child that shyness is an excuse for getting out of uncomfortable situations.

- Talk about ways your child can change the negative "self-talk" that accompanies shyness. How else might she interpret and, perhaps, channel her anxieties when she has to give a speech in a class or meet someone new?

- Help your child rehearse at home. Children gain confidence if they can try out behaviors that they perceive as fearful in a safe setting and with familiar people. Let your child practice making an upcoming classroom presentation, for example. Acknowledge that these things are difficult, but keep encouraging her.

Sexual Harassment

I remember the combination of fear and embarrassment in the voice of the fifteen-year-old girl as she told me about her ordeal on the school bus that had started earlier that year. Because she had red hair, several sixth-grade boys who rode the bus started calling her "fire crotch" as they giggled and snickered among themselves. She told them to stop, but that apparently only encouraged them.

The girl's sister, who had overheard the taunts, complained to the school bus driver, who said that there was nothing she could do. Her mother spoke to both the bus company and the school principal.

For several months nothing changed—until the mother started using the phrase *sexual harassment* in her conversations with bus company officials. The boys were assigned to the seat behind the driver and were told that if the name-calling happened again, they would not be allowed on the bus.

A generation ago, the behavior of the boys would have been written off as harmless adolescent teasing. In fact, many mothers and more than a few fathers can think back and remember something that happened to them that they may not have thought of as sexual harassment at the time. Such harassment may prevent children from choosing certain activities or classes. It may "poison the environment" and convey the idea that school isn't a safe or a just place.

Today harassing behavior is taken much more seriously by school officials and parents, especially after several successful lawsuits stemming from incidents ranging from name-calling to failure to erase graffiti on a bathroom wall.

But complaining is often difficult for adolescents—both boys and girls—even though both school policy and federal law are usually on their side. They worry about being labeled as tattletales or told that they have no sense of humor. To address protests to the harassers is to risk rejection when social acceptance by peers is often paramount. To complain to a school official is to risk embarrassment over issues that are already sensitive.

Sexual harassment of children by children is also a difficult topic for parents to talk about. The jump from harmless teasing to harassment is sometimes not obvious. The difference in status or power between the abuser and the victim—a hallmark of sexual harassment in the workplace—is often absent, or at least not as obvious to adults. It's easy to brush off the incidents as nothing more than youthful exuberance. Many parents who will respond strongly to an adult who's sexually harassing their child are less clear as to what they should do if it's a peer who's doing the harassing.

One reason adolescents harass their peers is because of their own insecurities about sexuality. When it occurs in a group, it has the function of showing off to other kids that you know something about sex even though, in reality, it shows that you know very little. (The twelve-year-old boy who started the taunting on the school bus was apparently trying to increase his status in front of his classmates by doing just that.)

Another reason for the harassment is that some of the models for adult and adolescent relationships—on television, in movies, or in popular music—are abusive and exploitative. To an adolescent, the wide exposure of such relationships in the mass media creates an aura of normalcy and appropriateness, especially if she doesn't see them being questioned and challenged by the adults around her.

Helping a Child Who's Been Harassed

Perhaps the most important information parents and teachers can give children who have been sexually harassed by their peers is that it's not their fault. They shouldn't feel that they deserve this or that they've done something wrong.

Here are some other things that adults can do to prevent the problem, or to handle it once it's occurred:

- Raise the issue ahead of time with your children, both boys and girls. Point out incidents of harassment that you see on television or in real life. Doing so could help your child to put such behavior in perspective and to know that you disapprove of it. You might even try role-playing a situation to encourage your children to think about how they might respond.

Talk to your child about the difference between flirting and harassment. Discuss how it feels really different when you get attention from someone you like versus when you don't want the attention.

- Talk about what your children should do if they're spectators. Remember that children are more likely to see harassment happening to someone else than to have it happen to them. Discuss how giggling, playing along, or even doing nothing can encourage the harassers to continue. Talk about what they might say to someone who is harassing a classmate. Remind your children that they don't have to intervene themselves if the situation is dangerous, and that they can and should call over a responsible adult, such as a teacher.

- Work with your child's school on developing and enforcing a formal policy on sexual harassment. Putting the policy in writing and discussing it with the children lets them know what behavior is unacceptable and will not be tolerated. Doing so also helps victims of harassment feel more comfortable talking to teachers or school administrators, since a policy would clearly state who is in the wrong and would give the children a way to make the harrassment stop.

5

Dating

Love is a disease which fills you with a desire to be desired.

—HENRI, COMTE DE TOULOUSE-LAUTREC (1864–1901)

Of all the social activities of adolescence, dating probably carries with it the most anxiety, confusion, and concern for both parents and children. Like so many other markers of development, the age at which children start to date is seldom of any consequence unless it's extremely early or late. In fact, while school-age children, teenagers, and adults may use the term *dating* to describe what they're doing, their activities may be quite different and reflect their respective stages of development and emotional maturity.

Let's begin with preteens to show how this works. I remember interviewing a psychology professor who described how he was no longer surprised when he answered his home telephone and heard several young girls giggling, followed by a quick *click* as they hung up. The calls weren't for him, of course. They were for his ten-year-old son.

The girls' awkward attempts at socializing—as well as their use of the telephone, which provides a marvelous combination of intimacy and anonymity—were right on schedule. Most of the telephone calls came on Friday nights, when the girls would gather at one another's homes and egg each other on to make the calls.[1]

As with many developmental issues, the girls were slightly ahead of the boys. The psychologist's son found the telephone calls embarrassing and vaguely disconcerting. Some of his male classmates, however, relished this new attention.

The young girls who used each other to gather the confidence they needed to place a telephone call to a boy were merely acting out their ambivalence over this first step toward dating. So was the embarrassed boy who received the calls. Both were testing the waters slowly before moving to the next step.

There's tremendous natural variation in how quickly children mature socially. While some want to "go steady" in elementary school, others show no interest in becoming emotionally involved and spending time with the opposite sex (or the same sex) until late in high school or beyond. Neither is, by itself, a cause for concern. Problems arise when children feel forced into a new role before they are ready.

Although an interest in befriending and dating the opposite sex is sometimes seen by parents as a measure of social maturity, child-development researchers disagree with that view. In fact, some precocious behaviors can lead to serious problems.

---

[1] These telephone calls also reflect something that many parents of both boys and girls are worried about: a change in the social aggressiveness of young girls. A generation or two ago it would have been highly unlikely that even an older teenage girl would have been as socially or even sexually aggressive as many adolescent girls are today. One reason may be the interpersonal behavior young children see modeled on television.

According to Dr. David Elkind of Tufts University, the real problem with early dating is that the child may bypass a stage of developing close friends of the same sex. That may interfere with developing more sophisticated heterosexual relationships when the child is older.

This has to do, in part, with how the nature of friendship changes as children mature. Children in early elementary school choose their friends largely based on convenience (they live next door or are in the same class) and shared activities such as sports and clubs. Most of their friends are of the same sex.

But around age ten, children begin selecting friends based on shared values, interests, and beliefs—choices that reflect their growing social skills and their increased ability to think abstractly. These are more complex and intimate relationships, which allow children to practice some of the new social skills they need when dating. If they rush into dating, they miss the opportunity to hone those important skills.

A child who begins one-on-one dating before the early teenage years is probably announcing that she isn't getting the emotional support, nurturing, or attention she needs at home. Unfortunately, these unmet needs set her up as someone to be easily manipulated by her dates.

There's also pressure from the mass media, especially television, for young children to date earlier. Many of the preteen and early-teen characters on popular television programs are shown dealing with adult issues, especially social relationships. That may give young viewers inappropriate expectations for how they should behave.

Music videos, television commercials, and print advertisements can also distort children's ideas of how they're expected to interact with the opposite sex. Even schools may unwittingly contribute to this premature push toward heterosexual relationships.[2]

The first thing you should do if you're trying to judge how ready your children are for dating is to look beyond their ages. Children who are immature, easily manipulated, or have poor self-esteem are at higher risk for being sexually or emotionally exploited when they date. That's why the decision to allow children to start dating should be based on the parents' values, as well as their insights into how well their children have formed more mature friendships with children of the same sex.

Children who see their friends acting seductively and wearing sexy clothing are under a lot of social pressure to do the same things. If they don't, they risk rejection by their same-sex friends—the group they need to be with. That's when parents' restrictions can feel welcome to teenagers—even though they may be loath to admit it. Having a parent who says "You can't go to that party" can give the adolescent an excuse that allows her to save face in front of her friends.

The Timing of Dating

Some parents are more nervous about their children's dating than the children are. There may, of course, be good reasons for this—especially if those children are likely to become sexually active. The risks of unprotected sex are significantly

---

[2] The father of an eleven-year-old girl told me that she was upset when she was invited to attend a school-sponsored dance on Halloween. What she really wanted to do, she said, was go out trick-or-treating with her girlfriends.

higher now than they were when today's parents were teenagers.

But in the beginning, sexual activity is seldom a concern. Here are some things to keep in mind when your children start showing an interest in the opposite sex:

- Don't panic if your child tells you he or she is going steady. During late elementary school and middle or junior high school, claiming to have a boyfriend or girlfriend often has much more to do with impressing the child's friends of the same sex than with going out on dates. Most of the time when children this age say they're going steady with someone, it's mostly talk, not romance.

- Don't worry if your child isn't interested in dating at the same age you were. Remember that there's tremendous natural variation in children's interest in the opposite sex. As with most aspects of child development, a strong interest in dating is only a concern if it occurs several years ahead of or after your child's peers.

  What's more important is that your child have the social skills she needs to build other friendships. A teenager who doesn't have enough self-esteen to engage in a same-sex friendship is crying out for professional help.

  Keep in mind that your child's emotional response to this situation is more important than yours. If your child is upset about not dating, then it's an issue you should explore together. If she isn't upset, don't force the issue.

- Pay attention to the messages you give your children about dating. Children look to their parents for subtle cues about whether they may confide their confusing feelings about dating. If children sense that their parents will quickly judge, criticize, or reject them, they'll try to hide what they're doing and how much they're feeling. Parents who are anxious about their children's social life may unintentionally give them the message that they can't talk about it.

  One approach is to share some of your own early dating (or nondating) experiences with your child. Talk about your emotions at the time, for that will let your child know she's not the only one to have felt strongly about this, and give her permission to share what she's feeling.

- Use phone calls from members of the opposite sex to teach your child some new social skills. Some children feel caught in a bind when this happens. They want to maintain some sort of relationship with the person who's calling, but they don't feel comfortable with a greater degree of intimacy. You can talk about—and even role-play, if your child doesn't feel too embarrassed—how to handle getting a telephone call from someone when she doesn't want to speak with him at that time.

- Remember the true purpose of dating during adolescence. Dating is a way for children to try out new and more adult social roles as they make the transition to independence. Any experience that allows a child to test these more mature roles will serve that purpose. Going out in mixed-sex groups or going to mixed-sex social events is often more important developmentally for adolescents than dating as a couple.

- Don't base your decision on when to let your children date on what others their age are doing. Emotional maturity and comfort are much more important indicators of when they're ready. Children sometimes need your permission to act like kids a little longer.

  This can sometimes be difficult, since parents may feel their own social pressure to let their children date. But if you feel that your child isn't ready, you should take a stand and try to find parents who have similar feelings. The lessons you teach your child by doing this will extend well beyond the issues of dating.

- Don't push your children to date. Doing so will probably backfire, especially if your children are anxious about it. Instead, encourage them to become involved in mixed-sex activities that don't seem as risky. Working together on a school play or a yearbook, or participating in a community project gives teenagers a chance to test new ways of socializing without feeling that everything they do is being judged by the opposite sex.

Preparing for the First Date

Experimenting with adult-style, one-on-one dating is a major step for many adolescents. It's a way for them to announce to the people around them, as well as to themselves, that they are ready for new relationships and social roles that go beyond those of childhood. It's also a way for them to learn more about who they really are and how they are perceived by others when they are outside the bounds of school and home.

Going out on a first date can be a very important event in a teenager's life for other important reasons. It signifies that the child has been deemed acceptable and desirable company by someone else—two key issues in their stage of development. It also changes the child's status among her peers, and sometimes within her family as well.

Few children take the plunge into such social activities without first testing the waters in larger groups. In many parts of the world, children begin attending coeducational parties and school dances when they reach early adolescence. Yet most of the interaction that takes place at these early parties is clearly divided by gender, with boys spending most of their time talking to other boys, and girls doing the same with girls.[3]

That discomfort and awkwardness usually continues for a few years or longer as the teenagers progress to group dates and double dates. According to Dr. Laurence Steinberg, a professor of

---

[3] I still remember both the awkwardness and the feelings of terror that accompanied me to my first few school dances. It's hard to recall which was more disconcerting: facing rejection or, perhaps even worse, obvious indifference when it was the boys' turn to ask the girls to dance; or waiting what seemed like forever to see if a girl—any girl—would ask me when it was the girls' turn. Although everyone else in the room seemed unfazed by this, I now know that we were each suffering in silence.

psychology at Temple University who studies adolescent development, the average age at which American children from middle-
class neighborhoods have their first one-on-one date is fourteen
to fifteen for girls and fifteen to sixteen for boys. Other researchers have found that children from poorer neighborhoods tend to
begin dating earlier.

Perhaps the largest factor influencing when children first date,
however, is the school they attend. Individual schools convey specific but differing social expectations to students. Adolescents
tend to start dating according to the cultures of their schools
more than the cultures of their homes.[4]

Dating later than one's classmates appears to be more of an
emotional stressor for girls than for boys. Girls who haven't
started dating by around age seventeen may begin feeling that
they're not socially desirable or acceptable. They're convinced
that everyone else their age is dating—even though there's clear
evidence that that's simply not true.

Teenagers who are new to dating are usually unsure of themselves and unclear on how they should behave. Many look to the
mass media for hints on what would be romantic. Despite the
relationships modeled on television programs, music videos, and
current films, a surprising number of young teenagers adopt a
style of behavior that is at once both reassuring and disconcerting
to their parents.

Their actions on these first dates are often highly stereotyped,
as if they were drawing from the script of a Doris Day–Rock

---

[4] It's important to remember that with dating, as with other markers of development such as toilet
training and walking, a few years later it will be almost impossible to tell when a child first attempted
it. The only exceptions might be those children at the extremes—the ones who started many years
ahead of or (more likely) behind their peers.

Hudson movie from the 1950s. For girls, that means taking a passive role with respect to initiating the date and deciding how they should spend the time, even if those girls are usually highly assertive. For boys, the script is the opposite, even if that doesn't feel very comfortable. For parents who have been trying to foster more egalitarian roles, this can be very confusing and even upsetting.[5]

Much of this stereotyped behavior can be attributed to teenagers' acute concerns about the judgments of their peers. A girl may hesitate to ask a boy out for fear that her friends may see it as proof that no one finds her attractive. A boy may feel flustered when his date insists on paying for her half of the pizza or for her own movie ticket if he thinks she is questioning his masculinity, or if he believes his friends will view him as less self-reliant and more immature.

Those fears are usually unfounded, of course. You can help your children become more comfortable with less-stereotyped roles by discussing what types of behaviors teenagers can expect from themselves and their dates.

The challenge of dating can be daunting to adolescents, especially since their growing skill at empathy makes them particularly vulnerable to feelings of embarrassment. Their new role as "date" brings with it, among other things, a need for social graces they may seldom have practiced. After all, if you're in a restaurant with your parents, they may put up with your being sulky. But if you're on your first date, you realize that someone has to make conversation and carry it along.

---

[5] One mother I interviewed—a very aggressive and successful advertising executive—described the beginning of her fifteen-year-old daughter's first date: "He came to the door and waited for her to descend the staircase." It reminded me of the chiffon-draped opening of the 1950s era *Loretta Young Show* on television in which she started each program with much the same affectation.

Parents' Tips for Before That First Date

There are several things you can do to help your children make a smooth (or at least a smoother) transition to one-on-one dating:

- Be sensitive to your child's awkwardness and discomfort, especially in the beginning. One of the reasons teenagers like dating is that it helps them feel mature. But grilling your child in front of his date about where they're going and what they'll do undermines those feelings and breeds resentment. Instead, try to get that information ahead of time when you're alone with your child.

  For similar reasons don't interpret your child's reluctance to discuss what happened on a recent date as an indication that things went poorly. One of the privileges of adulthood is privacy. Your child may interpret your desire to share information and feelings as nosiness and an attempt to put him back in a more childlike role.

- Empower your children to make decisions on their own. Remind them that they always have a choice about when they start dating. Let them know that they don't have to do things they don't want to and that part of your job as a parent is to help them figure out what's right for them.

  This goes well beyond sexual issues and behaviors. Remember that teenagers don't equate early dating with having sex. Other social issues are more important at that time. Also keep in mind that if you allow your children to talk about sexuality and the feelings they may have about their dates, you'll make it easier for them to ask questions without feeling embarrassed.

• Expect your children to ask questions about what you did when you were their age. Many parents find this awkward—especially if you were engaging in behaviors that you don't feel are right for your own children. Think ahead of time about what you wish to share and what you wish to keep private so that you're not making those decisions under the pressure of the moment.

The Ritual of Prom Night

When I wrote a *New York Times* column about senior proms a few years ago, I interviewed two teenagers who were preparing for two very different experiences. The boy had been eagerly awaiting his senior prom for months. He'd saved his money from an after-school job so that he could rent a tuxedo, share the cost of a stretch limousine, and pay for his and his date's formal dinner, all-night party, and sunrise breakfast on the beach.

The girl and her classmates had decided to do a parody of the traditional prom. Theirs would be an all-girl affair, complete with funky clothes and tacky decorations. It would be held at five in the afternoon in the school's cafeteria. (When pressed, however, she admitted that she and many of her classmates would also be attending traditional senior proms at other schools.)

The prom, whether it's done with tongue in cheek or hand in wallet, is a rite of passage for many high school seniors. It's a time to celebrate the end of one period of life and the beginning of opportunities and responsibilities that lie ahead. Like most rituals, it involves behavior that in other circumstances would be prohibited or that, at the very least, would appear out of place. Teenagers who have never partied all night or seen the sunrise with a date will get their first chance to do so.

But proms can also present new problems for adolescents, as well as aggravate exisiting ones. They are a cause of increased concern among educators and parents, who worry about the growing emphasis on materialism, about peer pressure to use alcohol and other drugs and to engage in sexual activities, and about issues of safety, especially the dangers of driving while under the influence of alcohol. Parents are caught between wanting to help their children celebrate this important transition in their lives and wanting to protect them from the dangers of that celebration if things get out of control.

For many families, however, the most problematic aspect of attending a prom is the pressure for the child to spend a lot of money. In some high schools it's not unusual for a boy to spend up to one thousand dollars or more for clothing, dinner, and transportation, and for a girl to spend almost as much on a prom dress and other preparations for the evening. This is a striking increase from a generation ago, even taking inflation into account.

This new emphasis on money may mean that what used to be a school and community celebration has been turned into a discriminatory and potentially destructive event. In some communities, those children from affluent families can set a standard few classmates can attain. Status is measured by the length of the limousine or the size of the dinner check. Simply having fun and blowing off some steam is not good enough. The rite of passage is now for a select few instead of all the children at the school, since some of the teenagers are doing it "right" and others are doing it "wrong."

Preparing for the Prom

There are several things you can do to help your children prepare for a prom. Even though it's a very special occasion for many teenagers, it's not a time for you to abdicate your authority or responsibility as a parent—although it calls for a gentle hand and a recognition of the importance of the event. Here are some suggestions:

- Set limits. Let your children know they shouldn't cave in because of peer pressure. In fact, showing your own resistance in the face of social pressure may help your children feel more comfortable resisting the peer pressure they're feeling.

- Help your children look at the consequences of their behavior. Recognize that telling teenagers that spending a few hundred dollars on a stretch limousine with two moon roofs is a waste of money will probably only make them defensive about their decision. (Of course it wasn't a *logical* decision—nor should it have been. Part of the point of a prom is getting a chance to play a caricature of a sophisticated adult, if only for an evening.)

Instead, help your children see that spending all that money on the limo means that they may not have enough money to do the things they want during the summer. Work out the calculations with them. See if they can come up with alternatives to their current plans.

- Talk about peer pressure. Many teenagers are unsure of what behavior is expected of them, especially during the time immediately preceding and immediately following the prom. They look to their peers for clues to how they should behave and which rites of passage they must pass through. The pressure to conform can be intense. Heavy drinking, drug use, sex, and even date rape are more likely to occur in the presence of such pressures.

  Acknowledge to your children that it's easy to get into a bad situation when they're trying to keep up with their friends. But emphasize that they need to do what's important to *them* instead of what their friends want. Agree on limits to their behavior, and practice ways they can respond to social pressure that makes them uncomfortable.

- Reduce the risk. Talk to your child (and to other parents) about alternative ways of celebrating immediately after the official prom. Your goal here is to maintain the excitement that goes along with this celebration, but to minimize the risks associated with drugs and drunk driving. Remember that whatever you choose, it can't be too tame, or it won't be attractive.

- Finally, encourage your children not to drive, even if they promise you they won't drink. It's not worth the risk. If their prom plans require a car and they can't afford to share the cost of a limousine for the evening, help them to make the payment, to modify their plans, or arrange for an adult such as an older brother or sister (parents just won't do in this situation) to act as a chauffeur in a rental car.

When You Don't Like Your Teenager's Date

No parent expects to like all of his or her children's dates. Yet there are times when those relationships strike a particularly dissonant chord. To parents' eyes, the mismatch may seem obvious: He's too old for her. She acts disrespectfully. He belittles her. She's not mature enough to handle the relationship, or perhaps to be dating at all.

Adolescents often view their budding romances quite differently than adults do. They may also respond to their parents' comments in ways that upset both generations by reacting hysterically or showing even greater determination to maintain the relationship.

An acquaintance of mine says she still cringes when she recalls how her oldest daughter, then fourteen, secretly started dating. Neither she nor her husband felt comfortable with the boy, since he wasn't from their neighborhood and they knew nothing about him—reasons they now recognize were little more than a reaction to their child's growing independence. They also thought their daughter was simply too young for one-on-one dating.

The mother—who happens to be a psychologist who specializes in working with teenagers—says that she was so angry and upset by her daughter's behavior that she lost her perspective and responded on a purely emotional level. ("I wanted to ground her until she was thirty" were her exact words.)

Although her protective feelings were understandable, she soon realized that in the short term her attempts to stop her daughter's involvement may have done more harm than good. Several studies have shown that attempts to keep the young couple apart simply make them find each other more attractive. The more the parents oppose the relationship, the more intense it becomes.

Dating during adolescence serves a different purpose than dating during young adulthood. The teenage years are a time of experimentation and separation from the family. The two are intricately intertwined, since it is easier for a teenager to test his independence from his parents if he feels emotionally intimate with someone else. That newfound intimacy provides a kind of emotional safety net.

Adolescence is also a time of intense social pressures. Just as high school students may try to distance themselves from the superficial aspects of their parents' values through the way they dress and the music they listen to, they try with equal enthusiasm to blend in with their classmates. For many teenagers, having a steady boyfriend or girlfriend helps them fit into that larger social group. It almost doesn't matter who that person is.

Even though they may not be very serious about the people they are dating, teenagers pay close attention to their parents' reactions. Because they are struggling with issues related to separation from their family, they may interpret a parent's negative or offhand comment about a date as an attack on their own maturity or independence.

This is one of the areas in which adolescents seemingly have supersensitive ears that pick up the slightest hint of a parent's criticism. Despite their outward bravado, many are emotionally fragile, and tend to overinterpret comments as criticism rather than caring. After all, a date may be the first person whom your teenager feels really cares about her socially. That's why if you make any comments about that person, you'll meet with strong resistance unless you acknowledge the importance of that person to your child.

Despite the intensity of these early relationships, they seldom last. This is especially true for children who are college-bound, since they tend to marry later. But for all adolescents, the importance of dating lies less in discovering the other person than in finding out about themselves. Dating at this age isn't just about love or passion. It's about growing up and becoming an independent adult.

Handling a Problem Date

So, what do you do and say when your son or daughter wants to go out with someone who isn't quite up to your hopes and aspirations? Here are some things to keep in mind:

- Often the best thing to do is nothing. Remember that most of these relationships are transient. Pushing to end one can make a teenager cling to that person even more tightly. You should ask yourself how intense the relationship is. If they've only dated once or twice, you should probably not say anything and trust your child's good judgment to end the relationship.

- Pay attention to what's really triggering your reaction to your child's date. Sometimes parents are surprised by their immediate and strong reaction when their child's date comes from a different religion, race, or social background. Even though such differences are the basis for your response—a reaction your child may be testing by dating this person—you may find yourself searching for other, more socially acceptable ways to explain your initial feelings toward this person. Instead, take a look at why you feel this way, and try not to project those feelings onto the date.

    It's also easy to fall into the trap of judging someone simply on the basis of dress or grooming—for example, a boy who wears earrings or a girl with too much makeup. Also, standards applied to twenty-five-year-olds may be misleading when applied to teenagers who are still trying to develop their identities.

- Don't stand by if your child's in an abusive relationship. (I'll discuss this later in this chapter.) Keep in mind that this is a judgment that the parent, not the child, should make, since adolescents and even adults sometimes have trouble recognizing when they're being abused.

  If you suspect that your child is being physically or psychologically mistreated, you should talk to your child about what a good relationship is really like. Don't hesitate to step in and say that you don't want her to go out with this person. Help your children understand that they shouldn't hang around with people who make them feel bad about themselves.

- When talking about your child's date, focus on specific behaviors rather than personality characteristics. If you begin with personality issues, your child will probably become defensive and tune you out.

  Instead, begin by talking about the things that you (honestly) do like about the date. State that you can see why your child would be attracted to this person. Then talk about the specific things you would appreciate this other person doing, either toward your child or toward you, such as not walking into your house unannounced or not telephoning late at night.

- Ask your child what she finds attractive about this person. One of two things may result from this conversation. You may discover hidden aspects of the date's personality and behavior that will help you feel more comfortable with him. Or, your child may use this as a springboard for discussing some of the things about him that bother her as well.

- Be sensitive to good motives for getting into bad relationships. Sometimes teenagers will become involved with people who have serious problems in the unrealistic belief that they can turn that person's life around. If you suspect that your child is trying to "save" this person, talk about how hard it is for an adult to do that, much less a teenager. Help your child figure out other ways she could help, such as by referring her friend to an appropriate drug clinic or mental health center.

Abusive Relationships

A psychologist I interviewed described a teenager she was treating. Although the girl was only seventeen years old, she had been dating the same boy for four years. But she'd grown tired of his hitting her, and wanted to end the relationship. He'd told her that if she tried to break up with him, he'd kill her. She believed him (apparently with good reason), but hadn't told her parents, who had sent the girl to the psychologist because her grades at school were slipping.

While death threats are extreme, a surprisingly large number of teenage girls become involved in abusive relationships. Research by Dr. Eva Feindler at Long Island University has found that up to 30 to 40 percent of teenage girls in the United States have been hit at least once by their boyfriends or dates. Most of the abuse occurs during long-term relationships. Parents rarely know it's going on unless there are visible bruises. It's a topic that teenage girls seldom bring up, even if they have a good relationship with their parents.

For many of these children, this is a pattern of victimization and denial that starts in their own families and, if they aren't helped, continues throughout their lives. The ones who are victimized the most—that is, those who get into a series of abusive relationships—are likely to have come from homes where the parents are physically, verbally, or sexually abusive to each other or to the children. Family violence is part of their everyday experience. They grow up assuming that such mistreatment is normal and may even be a sign of love.

The risks go beyond just that. Research by Dr. Arthur H. Green at the Columbia University College of Physicians and Surgeons found that children who are physically abused are at greater risk of marrying people who will abuse them as adults. Also, girls who have been sexually abused are at greater risk of getting involved with men who will sexually abuse their children.

Children from these families usually have very low self-esteem and feel socially inadequate. They believe their abusers, who tell them that they've brought the attacks on themselves by nagging or questioning. Many of these teenagers have what's known as victim thinking. They say to themselves, "I must deserve this. I'm lucky to have anyone at all."

Many of the abusers come from similar environments. They also have poor self-images and underdeveloped social skills. For them, an insecure adolescent is a safe target for their anger and lack of emotional and physical control.

A teenager who is mistreated by only one of her dates usually has a different background. Her family is often warm and supportive. She hasn't been abused at home. Yet she may justify the brutality of her boyfriend by saying that she's trying to help him. She may see herself as a savior and interpret the abuse as the price she must pay for her noble deeds.

But this desire to be helpful no matter what the cost is also a sign of underlying insecurities. While she talks of her boyfriend's emotional needs, she denies her own. By doing so, she makes herself an easier target for more mistreatment.

Both types of victims have difficulty seeing the patterns of abuse. They tend to treat each assault as an isolated case—an aberration that should be excused with a little understanding and patience. They feel that if there's a problem, it must be their own fault.

Helping a Child Who's in an Abusive Relationship

Discovering that your child has been physically or emotionally abused by a date can bring out a parent's rawest emotions. But that protectiveness is likely to backfire unless you take into account your child's state of mind and emotional development.

You can't just say, "Stop seeing that boy!" In fact, that may draw them closer together. Even if it does work, you haven't addressed the underlying issues, so your child's next relationship may be abusive as well.

Here are some things you should remember if your child's a victim:

- Don't fly off the handle. Your child's already very worried about being rejected. If you're angry, she will have difficulty listening beyond that anger to your words. Instead, ask her to tell you what's going on. Find out if she wants the relationship to stop. What makes her feel that things might change?

  By listening without criticizing, you'll not only find out how realistic your child's appraisal of the situation is, you'll also let her know that you value her thoughts and feelings.

  Also, don't give the appearance of taking charge of the situation right away. If your child is feeling powerless and victimized, and you run in and take over, that will make her feel even more powerless.

- Talk about the choices she has. Many victims of abuse feel so trapped that they don't look for alternatives to their situation. Let her know that she doesn't deserve this type of relationship and doesn't have to stay in it.

  Tell her that if she wants to walk away from the relationship and she's afraid, you'll protect her. If you're concerned for your daughter's safety, part of that protection may require using the police and the courts.

- Look for professional help for your child. Remember that accepting the abuse is usually a reflection of a deeper problem. Parents are too emotionally involved with their children to offer the best help by themselves.

Sharing a Broken Heart

The breakup of an older adolescent's long-term relationship can be very painful, for the child and occasionally for the parent as well. We may vicariously feel our child's hurt, disappointment, and anger. It is, at best, an awkward situation. Yet this experience may provide parents and children with an opportunity to learn about one another at a different level and begin a new stage of their relationship.

In the late 1980s Dr. Terri L. Orbuch, a social psychologist at the University of Michigan in Ann Arbor, studied 150 college students and nonstudents to find out how they handled the breakup of long-term relationships. She found that late adolescents were more likely to go to their friends for support than to their parents because, they said, they thought their friends would take their situation more seriously.

One of her most striking findings was the differences in the ways men and women tended to handle the stress of the breakup.

Women this age were more likely to seek advice from family members and friends. Men were more likely to respond to the breakup by spending more time in competitive sports.

Other studies have indicated the tendency of young women to be more verbal and young men more physical in their attempts to recover from broken relationships. While this may sound strikingly similar to the way boys and girls in early elementary school handle stressful events, this time it can't be attributed largely to differences in verbal skills.

Instead, it seems to be linked to how they feel others will respond to their descriptions of what happened. Young women describe sharing the story of their breakup as something that helps them grow closer to their peers because they feel more comfortable sharing such intimacies. Young men tend to be much less comfortable talking to each other this way. They may view the breakup as a failure on their part, and therefore a poor reflection on themselves.

You also shouldn't assume that men bounce back more easily than women from a love affair gone sour, or that women are more likely to be "dumped" than men. Research by Dr. Charles T. Hill of Whittier College in California found that several of the commonly held assumptions about the differences between how men and women perceive relationships are false. Starting in the mid-1970s, he followed 231 college-age couples who said that they were seeing each other exclusively. He found that 50 percent had broken up within fifteen years.

But unlike the stereotype that men are the ones to end most relationships, Dr. Hill found that in his sample, women were more likely to be the ones to break up with their partners. He and others have also found that men were more likely to hold starry-eyed beliefs such as that true love lasts forever and that love can overcome all obstacles.

Finally, there are certain times of year when young love is likely to come to an end and therefore when parents are more likely to see its ramifications. Studies of long-term teenage relationships have found that young couples tend to break up at the beginning or end of the school year, or over Christmas break. These are, perhaps, the easiest times to end a relationship because the changes in an adolescent's schedule increase the likelihood of quickly meeting another potential partner.

Responding to the Breakup

Parents of adolescents who have just broken up with their long-term boyfriend or girlfriend should keep several things in mind when talking to their children about the situation:

- Don't rush in with advice. Many parents feel uncomfortable in this situation because it reminds them of painful episodes from their own adolescence. Remember that a breakup can be like a death, and a teenager (and an adult as well) may need to go through a certain amount of mourning to resolve it.

  Giving advice will probably make your child feel worse because it sets the two of you up in old roles, and may emphasize his feelings of inadequacy or incompetence. Instead, acknowledge what he is saying and let him know what emotions you are hearing in his voice. This lets him know that you are listening, and helps him think through the situation.

• Gently encourage your child to discuss how he feels about himself after a breakup. This is particularly important for young men, since many feel uncomfortable disclosing emotions, especially those that could be interpreted as signs of weakness.

If your child doesn't want to talk, don't try to force the issue. Let your child take the initiative to express his feelings in his own way. Applying too much pressure before your child is ready will make him even more hesitant to discuss the problem. Instead, tell him that you're available if he wants to talk.

Don't worry if your child never talks to you about the situation. That simply means that he felt more comfortable, at that moment, confiding in someone else.

• Don't dismiss or deny the significance of the relationship. In an effort to be reassuring, parents sometimes say things like, "By the time you're thirty, you'll have forgotten all about this." But diminishing the problem will probably make your child feel worse since he now feels rejected by his parents as well. Besides, by the time he's thirty, he will *not* have forgotten all about his relationship; he simply will have changed his perspective on it.

- Keep your opinions of the former girlfriend (or boyfriend) to yourself. It's tempting to lash out at the person associated with your child's pain. But keep in mind that people who have recently broken up, especially adolescents, often have ambivalent feelings about each other. If you criticize the former boyfriend, your child may feel even more uncomfortable and may begin to defend the other person.

6

Risky Behaviors: Alcohol, Drugs, Smoking, and Sex

There is no vice so simple but assumes some mark of virtue on his outward parts.

—WILLIAM SHAKESPEARE, *The Merchant of Venice*, III.ii.

Much of childhood is marked by experimentation, including the search for altered states of consciousness. A five-year-old spins until dizzy. An eight-year-old sits transfixed in front of a video game. By the time children reach early adolescence, that normal experimentation can take a dangerous turn.

According to a 1992 national survey by the Institute for Social Research at the University of Michigan, approximately 70 percent of eighth-grade students say they've used alcohol, and 27 percent admit they've been drunk. The next most popular drugs among children this age were cigarettes (45 percent), smokeless tobacco (21 percent), and marijuana or hashish (11 percent).

It's not easy for parents to know how to prevent or even respond to drug and alcohol experimentation. It is especially difficult for those parents who came of age during times of sexual and drug experimentation in the 1960s and 1970s. The concerns and risks are very different now from what they were a generation ago. Convincing today's young people of that, however, can be a difficult problem, particularly for parents who don't wish their children to follow in the footsteps they made during their own teenage years.

As I mentioned in Chapter 4, Friends and Peer Pressure, simplistic approaches such as "Just say no!" are often ineffective and may even backfire. Many drug-abuse researchers, while emphasizing that alcohol, cigarettes, and other drugs pose a major problem for abusers and the people around them, also state that seeking altered states of consciousness is normal and healthy. The real challenge is directing that need for experimentation into less self-destructive areas, especially for adolescents at greatest risk of becoming drug abusers.

The difference between experimentation with drugs and abuse isn't simply a matter of the amount used. Rather, it has to do with whether the drugs are becoming a substitute for other activities and meaningful relationships. To many researchers and clinicians, the important question isn't what leads teenagers to experiment with drugs and alcohol. It's what differentiates those who become addicts and abusers from the majority of children who experiment and don't get into trouble—either because they quit, or they learn to use those drugs (such as alcohol) in socially sanctioned ways.

One answer to that question may come from longitudinal research conducted by Dr. Jack Block and his colleagues at the University of California at Berkeley. They followed forty-nine boys and fifty-two girls from age three. When those children were eighteen years old, 20 percent were frequent marijuana users.

These teenagers showed significantly more social alienation, poor impulse control, and more emotional distress than adolescents who reported that they were experimenting with marijuana but not using it or other drugs frequently. Interestingly, they also found that those adolescents who, by age eighteen, had never experimented with any drug were relatively anxious, emotionally constricted and lacking in social skills.[1]

When the researchers looked at videotapes of the families and reports of the children's early behavior, they found that they were able to predict which children would get into trouble with drugs and which would not. Those children who were later to become heavy drug users had trouble forming relationships, were insecure, and showed numerous signs of emotional distress as early as age seven. Their mothers also tended to be more critical and hostile, and less protective than the norm. (The fathers showed no differences.)

Apparently the long-standing emotional problems of those adolescents, not just peer pressure, played a large part in their becoming drug abusers rather than normal teenage experimenters. This finding points to the need to help children early who are having psychological problems, rather than ignoring those prob-

---

[1] Dr. Block and his colleagues emphasize that their finding that the best-adjusted group of adolescents contained those who experimented with but did not abuse drugs should not be misinterpreted to imply that the use of those drugs *caused* the better social and emotional adjustment. Their data simply show that occasional experimentation with certain drugs need not lead to abuse or addiction.

They add that we have to remember that those teenage and adult drug abusers and alcoholics who present themselves for treatment are not representative of the general population of adolescents and adults. The psychological meaning of drug use is very different for this group. Their drug abuse is part of a larger set of problems.

lems in the hope that they will disappear as the child matures. It also means that programs to prevent drug abuse that focus largely on resisting peer pressure may be providing the least benefit to those children who are at greatest risk.

One behavioral sign that can help parents recognize teenagers who are more likely to become abusers is how adolescents handle privacy. Those children at greatest risk tend to be insistent about maintaining their privacy in nearly all areas of their lives. Teenagers who aren't abusers want their privacy as well, but they also desperately want to share what's going on in their lives with their parents. They want their parents' respect as well.

Another difference is how they assert their independence. Most teenagers are ambivalent about this issue, and seek a combination of autonomy and protection. Adolescents who abuse drugs don't vacillate between those conflicting desires. Instead they just keep moving farther and farther away from their parents emotionally, and become increasingly unreachable.

Helping Avoid Drug Abuse

While almost all adolescents find some way to experiment with altered states of consciousness, there are things that you can do to improve the odds that your children will focus on ways that don't involve alcohol and drugs. Here are some suggestions:

- Pay attention to what you do as well as what you say. In fact, your own behavior will have more influence on your children's choices in this and many other matters than your words. If you drink alcohol every evening to relieve your feelings of stress, or regularly take pills to help you handle anxiety, those lessons will be learned by your children.

- Provide your children with information about alcohol and drugs. Talk about both the pros and the cons. (Drinking alcohol may help you feel less inhibited, but you may do things that embarrass you, such as vomiting in front of your friends.) If you just talk about the bad things, that will encourage your child to lie to you about drug use. It will also push him to hide his behavior, which may lead to continued drug use.

  You should talk to your child about your values and the basis for your advice on drug and alcohol use. Let your child know that even "safe" drugs, such as alcohol, can be deadly to experiment with, either by overdosing or by leading to dangerous behavior such as driving while drunk or having unprotected sex.

- Let your child know that you're interested and available to talk about the topic whenever he wants. As with sex education, don't assume that programs to prevent drug abuse are giving your child all the information he wants or needs. If you leave it up to the schools or to your child's friends to provide information about experimenting with high-risk activities, he may get into more trouble than if you speak about it openly at home.

- Talk about what your child might be looking for by using alcohol or other drugs. If he's feeling shy or awkward at parties, how else might he become more self-confident?

- Look for other ways your child can find altered states of consciousness without using drugs. Remember that teenagers are looking for ways to test themselves physically and mentally. They're also trying to differentiate who they are now from who they were as little children. Sports such as skiing, rock climbing, or scuba diving can provide adolescents with a bit of a thrill and a feeling of power—the same sensations many are trying to get from drugs.

Decisions About Alcohol

For many families, drinking alcohol is a way to celebrate something. The good cheer of the holiday season is liberally laced with wine. We use Champagne and liquor to show our happiness at weddings and births.

This association of alcohol with celebration leads many parents to wonder whether or when they should permit their children to drink socially, even though it is illegal. Will forbidding alcohol make it even more appealing? Will condoning drinking lead to alcoholism for the child? If you talk to your child about not drinking and driving, is that giving him tacit permission to drink as long as he doesn't drive?

Alcoholism researchers and developmental psychologists say the answers are not that simple. They also agree that it's a bad idea to allow your children to drink alcohol at home simply because you assume they will just do it elsewhere. In fact, that makes it harder for teenagers to decline a drink in other situations. Protecting children from alcohol abuse requires a grasp of how different their thinking is from adult thinking, and recognition that alcohol can be a serious problem for them and their friends.

The nationwide laws against drinking alcohol by anyone under age twenty-one do little to prevent teenagers from obtaining it easily. Research by Dr. Henry Wechsler at the Harvard School of Public Health has found that about 40 percent of boys in their senior year of high school in the United States are binge drinkers—that is, when they drink, they have five or more drinks at a time. He's also found that among college freshmen, 80 percent of the men and 70 percent of the women admitted drinking alcohol within thirty days of being interviewed. Almost half the men and more than a third of the women said they'd been drunk during that time.

The allure of alcohol is strongest during adolescence, when many children are looking for ways to mask their feelings of awkwardness, bolster self-confidence, increase social acceptance, and take new risks. They have spent years developing expectations for what drinking alcohol will do and what it means. These images, which are often unrealistic, have been shaped in part by advertising and by their parents' patterns of drinking.

Studies by Dr. Alan Marlatt, the director of the Addictive Behaviors Research Center at the University of Washington at Seattle, have found that those teenagers who are most likely to have trouble with alcohol have different expectations of its risks and benefits. The high-risk adolescents expect that alcohol will always make them feel better and that the more they drink, the better they'll feel. They see it as a general tension reducer that will lower their social anxieties and concerns about self-esteem. Also, boys who are at high risk for alcohol abuse say that alcohol will make both them and their dates more attractive.[2]

Those adolescents at lower risk for abusing alcohol have a more balanced set of expectations, including concerns about getting sick and embarrassing themselves.

Avoiding Problems with Alcohol

Alcohol education should begin early for the simple reason that children are exposed to alcohol advertising well before they are old enough to drink. In fact, it's not unusual for preschoolers who see sports events and their accompanying commercials on television to be able to identify different brands of beer before they can read.

While you needn't start that early, it's a good idea to talk to your children about alcohol by early adolescence. Here are some approaches:

- Let your children know what you expect of them, and why. Simply saying you don't want him to drink won't convince a teenager unless you can back it up

---

[2] One teenager he interviewed told him that he drank heavily at parties because all of his dates "looked prettier through beer goggles."

with reasons. Giving your child clear expectations of family rules and an awareness of family values goes a long way. It means that when your child's confronted with peer pressure, he will know what you expect.

- Provide evidence for not wanting your child to drink alcohol. Ads show drinking as part of being a successful, competent, attractive adult—much as cigarette ads give the false impression that smokers are rugged athletes who have glistening white teeth and a broad range of physically attractive friends. Adolescents are especially susceptible to those messages. It provides what they want most at a time when they feel invulnerable to the risks involved.

  Point out stories in the newspaper where adolescents were involved in drunken-driving accidents or were arrested at public events or private parties for using alcohol. Don't do this all at once, but do it regularly and subtly.

- Pay close attention to your children's friends. Teenagers tend to drink what their friends do. If you know some of your child's friends are getting into trouble with alcohol, pay closer attention to your own child's behavior.

  Also, pay attention to and support your children's friendships with nondrinkers. An adolescent is more likely to refuse alcohol at a party if he is with a friend who also doesn't want to drink. The friend provides social support.

- Get to know the parents of your children's friends. Let them know you will not allow your underage children to attend parties where alcohol is served. Ask the other parents to agree to the same criteria.

- Talk to your child about not driving if he's been drinking, and about not getting into a car with a driver who's been drinking. Although some parents worry about this giving children a set of contradictory messages (i.e., you're not allowed to drink alcohol, but I expect that you will), it really does not.

  Instead, it allows your child to see your priorities: You have rules that you believe in, but you value his life and health more than any rule. Let your children know that if they call home from a party and say that they need to be picked up, you will either get them yourself or pay for a taxi to do so. Also, you will do this without questioning their motives or their integrity.[3] Giving your teenagers this power tells them that you trust their judgment, even if they make a mistake or get into trouble.

- Finally, recognize that two of the main reasons teenagers drink are to cope with stress and to experience an altered state of consciousness. Dr. Marlatt has found that college students who were heavy drinkers were able to reduce their alcohol consumption by 30 to 40 percent when they either did aerobic exer-

---

[3] This may come in handy in other situations as well, such as if you have a daughter who's worried about being sexually assaulted in her date's car on the way home. She'll feel much more comfortable calling you for help if she doesn't have to explain her reasons.

cise or practiced meditation. Those who regularly exercised and meditated reduced their alcohol consumption by 50 to 60 percent. Developing such alternative coping strategies might also prevent light drinkers from getting into trouble.

The Lure of Smoking

I realize that the heading for this section sounds melodramatic. Yet tobacco use in the United States, which has been steadily declining among adults and had been following the same trajectory among adolescents, has recently gone up significantly.

According to a series of annual surveys of fifty thousand American high school students by Dr. Lloyd D. Johnston at the University of Michigan's Survey Research Center, 18.6 percent of children in the eighth grade said that they'd smoked cigarettes within the previous thirty days in 1994. This was up from 14.3 percent in 1991. Among high school seniors, the numbers were 31.2 percent in 1994 compared with 27.8 percent in 1991. Even these disturbing percentages underestimate the true number of smokers, since they don't include teenagers who have dropped out of school and are therefore statistically more likely to smoke than teenagers who stay in school.

According to these and other surveys, children are more likely to smoke regularly if their friends and family members smoke, and if they are white. (The rate of daily smoking among black students is about half the rate among white students.) Students who have no plans for higher education are twice as likely to smoke as those who hope to attend a college or junior college.

School rules also appear to influence whether children smoke. School systems that allow smoking on their grounds graduate 25 percent more smokers per class than schools that don't. According to Dr. Joseph R. DiFranza of the University of Massachusetts, who has studied children's smoking, it's a myth that kids smoke in the school bathroom because they're trying to get away with something. He says the real reason has more to do with physiology than rebelliousness: They're undergoing nicotine withdrawal during English class and can't concentrate.

While roughly equal proportions of teenage boys and girls smoke regularly, their reasons are dramatically different. Boys often begin smoking as a way to demonstrate their maturity and masculinity, or to feel accepted by a particular clique.[4] Surveys of adolescent girls, however, have found that nearly all of them who smoke daily started doing so in an attempt to control their weight. (The true effect of smoking on weight control appears to be negligible, however.)

Some of the smoking-prevention programs offered to teenagers and younger children—especially those programs developed and distributed to schools and community groups by tobacco companies and related organizations—may actually backfire and make smoking more attractive to children.[5] By emphasizing smoking as "an adult choice," the programs subtly encourage adolescents to smoke cigarettes as a way of showing that they're no longer children.

---

[4] This attempt to gain social acceptability may lead to other problems. Studies by Dr. Robert C. Klesges at Memphis State University have found that both smoking and nonsmoking teenagers find smokers less attractive and are less interested in dating them.

[5] There are many of us who work in public health who believe that this is not an unintended effect on the part of the program developers. Rather, it is a very cynical form of manipulation. After all, these are the same people who promote cigarettes by using cartoon characters, yet claim that they are not trying to sell to children.

Helping a Child Quit or Not Start Smoking

Getting children to quit smoking, or persuading them not to start in the first place, can be more difficult than persuading an adult to do the same. Adolescents respond to different social pressures. The mind-set of invulnerability, living for the moment, and rebellion causes them to reject the arguments that lead many adults to stop smoking. The health warnings on cigarette packs and advertisements appear to have little effect on teenagers, who may see cigarettes as a way to lose weight, rebel, appear more mature, or fit into a particular social group.

Here are some suggestions for helping your child quit or not start smoking:

- Don't focus on long-term health hazards. Instead, talk about short-term effects, such as reduced athletic performance, bad breath, and yellow teeth. This can be an especially powerful argument to girls, who may start using cigarettes as a way of feeling more socially attractive.

- Find out how many of your children's friends smoke. Adolescents tend to dress and act the same as the people they spend time with. You may have to encourage your children to hang out with a different group. The more of the peer group that's smoking, the harder it will be for your children to break the habit.

- Appeal to your teenager's sense of righteous indignation. Adolescents hate to feel manipulated, which is
  why they will sometimes use cigarettes to rebel. Instead, talk to them about how the cigarette companies
  are manipulating them through their advertising.

  Also, don't present smoking as something that's for
  adults. That will make any kid want to do it. A better
  approach is to tell adolescents that they're old enough
  to know better, not that they're too young to smoke.[6]

Sex and Sexuality

I remember talking to a friend of mine who confided that she was
completely taken aback and, for a moment, left speechless when
her eleven-year-old daughter asked how old she should be before
having sex. My friend was a child psychiatrist. In fact, she was the
director of a program in human sexuality at a major university.
Still, she had not expected the question to come from her daughter's lips for at least two more years.

All parents are at least a little uncomfortable discussing matters of sexuality with their children. These discomforts often become more acute when those children reach adolescence and the
issues are no longer theoretical.

---

[6] I tried this out one evening when I ran into two boys about twelve years old who were sneaking a
smoke in an alleyway. Their grandiose gestures and great affectations with their cigarettes told me
that they were trying to appear mature and sophisticated. When I saw them, I said, "You know, with
those cigarettes in your mouths you guys look about eight years old."

This was clearly the opposite of the effect they were intending. They quickly snuffed out their
cigarettes and walked away. I don't know whether my comment had any lasting effect, but it clearly
got them to question some of their assumptions.

Discussions about sex take on a different tone than those about the other topics in this chapter. We may wish that our children never smoke or abuse drugs, but few of us would deny them the pleasures of exploring their sexuality—at an appropriate time and in an appropriate relationship.

When I was a member of the National Commission on Adolescent Sexual Health in 1994–95, we looked at what "normal" and "healthy" sexuality and sexual behavior was for this generation of American teenagers.[7] The findings were both reassuring and disturbing. Among them:

- By the time they are twenty years old, more than three quarters of adolescents have had sexual intercourse.

- Every year one million teenage girls become pregnant; more than a half million have a child; and three million teenagers acquire a sexually transmitted disease.

- Despite popular mythology and the inflammatory rhetoric of some politicians, the adolescent birthrate today is significantly lower than it was forty years ago. In 1955, ninety out of every thousand girls between the ages of fifteen and nineteen give birth. By 1992, that number had dropped to sixty-one out of every thousand teenage girls.[8]

- According to research by the Alan Guttmacher Institute and the U.S. Centers for Disease Control, the majority of teenag-

---

[7] The report of that commission, *Facing Facts: Sexual Health for America's Adolescents,* can be obtained from SIECUS Publications, 130 West 42nd Street, Suite 350, New York, N.Y. 10036–7802, for $12.95 including shipping.

[8] We must keep in mind that both women and men in the 1990s are marrying, on average, approximately three to four years later than women and men did in the 1950s. While the overall proportion of births to teenagers is lower in the 1990s than it was in the 1950s, the proportion of out-of-wedlock births to teenagers is significantly higher. According to the Alan Guttmacher Institute, in 1960–64 approximately one in three births to girls between the ages of fifteen and seventeen were out of wedlock. By 1985–89 that proportion had shot up to slightly more than eight out of ten.

ers who have had sexual intercourse have had only one partner. The majority of teenagers who have intercourse use contraception. Two thirds of adolescents use a contraceptive the first time they have intercourse, and more than three quarters do so on an ongoing basis. (This means, of course, that about 25 percent of adolescents are not using contraceptives regularly, putting them at risk not only for pregnancy but for sexually transmitted diseases each time they are not appropriately protected.)

To deny that adolescents have strong (and at times seemingly overwhelming) sexual feelings is to deny reality. At the same time, parents must not abdicate responsibility for helping their children come to terms with their sexual feelings.

Parents are the primary sexuality educators of their children. This is true despite the availability of sex-education courses in schools and the number of sexually explicit movies, television programs, and publications available to teenagers. Both by what they say and how they behave, parents teach their children how to interpret and understand their own and others' sexuality. In homes that have open and honest conversations about sex, young people tend to behave more responsibly. They are more likely to turn to their parents when they need help or information.

What's struck me the most from looking at scientific studies of teenager sexual behavior is that the children who become sexually active the earliest are generally the ones who have the *least* understanding of human sexuality. That's one of the main reasons to discuss the subject with your children honestly and openly (and at an appropriate level for their age). For example, if you talk about contraceptives before your children become sexually active, you're not only giving them potentially lifesaving information, but your openness may actually help delay when they start having intercourse.

It's never too late to start such conversations, even if your children have already become sexually active. Talk about the social pressure they feel—and which you felt as an adolescent. Is sexual intimacy a way for them to gain acceptance or to prove their maturity? What might be other ways for them to do those things? How can you say no to a date and still maintain the relationship? How can you say no if, on a previous date, you've said yes?

The challenge of teaching children about sex and sexuality has little to do with the mechanics of reproductive biology. For many adolescents, the most confusing aspects of sex have to do with emotions and responsiblities.[9] These can be far more difficult to discuss than fallopian tubes and erections. A child's failure to ask about sexual responsibility doesn't mean she knows all she needs to know. More likely, she senses her parents' discomfort with the issues.

But your feelings of discomfort can actually work to your advantage. By admitting that you are uneasy talking about the topic and asking for your children's patience and understanding, you are conveying how important the subject of sexuality is. You are also giving them permission to speak with you even if they, too, feel more than a bit uncomfortable.

---

[9] A colleague once told me that she knows a sex-education program will be ineffective when it emphasizes "plumbing" instead of other issues.

Talking About Sex

First of all, don't worry about whether you're going to be putting the topic of sex into your teenager's head. Rest assured that it's there already. What you can do through your discussions with your children is help them deal with the confusing and conflicting feelings brought about by their emerging sexuality.

Here are some ideas that can help:

- Have regular discussions about intimacy of all types, including emotional and sexual intimacy. Weave these into your regular conversations instead of saving them for isolated discussions. Don't talk about sex as a separate topic. Instead, help your children see it within a context of emotions.

- Use the plots of television programs and the lyrics of songs as springboards for conversations. What might happen if those two characters decided to have sex? What does the woman find attractive in that man? What do those lyrics mean to you? Does that make sense?

- Share some of your own experiences of when you first dated and first fell in love. Talk about the anxieties you had. Remember that each generation of adolescents feels as if it is the first to discover love and sex.

- Avoid preaching. In fact, you should probably listen more than you talk. It may help to talk about sex with more than one of your children at once. Remember that teenagers want to appear more sophisticated about sex than they really are. They'll often try to hide what they don't know. An eleven-year-old will freely ask some of the questions that a teenager feels afraid or embarrassed to ask.

- Let your children know what your values are. Teenagers in particular need a set of standards by which they can compare the values they are starting to try on for size.

- Let your children know that you respect their ability to make their own decisions about these issues. They'll probably live up to your expectations—whether those expectations are bad or good.

- Talk about sexual orientation. This is an especially confusing issue to adolescents—and to a great many adults as well. What does it mean to be homosexual? What are their (and your) feelings about people who are attracted to members of the same sex? How would you feel if your child were gay?

    This is not a topic to be glossed over. Adolescence is a time when children begin coming to terms with their sexuality, including their sexual orientation. Those teenagers who feel sexually "out of place" (especially those who conclude that their homosexual feelings will cause them to be rejected by their family) are at much greater risk for a variety of problems, including alcohol abuse and even suicide.

- Show your children that you will not reject them if they make a mistake. It's not a double message to tell teenagers that you prefer them not to have sexual intercourse, but if they're going to have intercourse, they must protect themselves.[10] You're sharing and emphasizing your values about premarital or adolescent sex, but you're also telling them that you value their lives more than you do conformity to those values.

Sexually Explicit Material

It was the phone bill that tipped off my friends. The charges for one morning's calls totaled $622, all made to a telephone sex line by their fourteen-year-old son and three of his classmates. The matter of the phone bill was quickly resolved.[11] But the parents faced a bigger issue: What do you do when your child sees or hears sexually explicit material that you feel could be upsetting or could lead the child to behave recklessly?

Experts on children's sexual development say that isolated incidents, such as watching a sexually explicit movie on cable television, buying a pornographic magazine, or trying a telephone sex line, are generally nothing to worry about. They simply reflect teenage curiosity and are part of normal adolescent development.

These situations can, however, provide parents with an oppor-

---

[10] Note that this is a similar situation to the issues related to drinking alcohol and driving.

[11] As in most cases like this when it's the first occurrence and involves a minor, the telephone company canceled the charges on the condition that the family accept an "electronic lock" on their telephone that would prevent additional calls to the 900-exchange.

tunity to talk about sexuality and values with their children. In deciding how to react, the age and emotional maturity of the child are almost always your best guide—even as to whether you should react at all. The type of sexual material or behavior you discover is less important than how you handle the situation.

The boys who called the 900 sex line needed one another's encouragement to do so. They were impressed that adult women would talk that way. As early adolescents, they were trying to discover what sexual relationships are all about and to figure out where they might fit in. Older teenagers, who are much more likely to place such calls while alone, know more about sexual relationships and are usually experimenting with eroticism. A parent who responds primarily to the fact that the child placed the call will miss this critical difference.

At least as important, but often overlooked, are the repeated messages about sexuality and sexual behavior that children see on afternoon and prime-time television. Teenage girls who are avid viewers of soap operas, for example, may develop an unrealistic and self-defeating approach to their own sexuality. For example, many of the young women on those programs aren't worried about AIDS or pregnancy; they're worried about being caught. (This makes for a better plotline—at least on television.) Teenage girls tend to mimic that concern, thereby putting themselves at greater risk.

Reacting to a Teenager's Erotic Experimentation

Discovering your child with sexually explicit materials need not be a traumatic experience for either generation. In fact, if it is handled well, it can lead to better and more open communication between you. Here are some suggestions:

- Don't feel you have to respond immediately. In fact, there are some advantages to waiting. Children who are embarrassed or angry are not going to be very receptive to anything you have to say. Similarly, if you show how upset you are, your children won't feel comfortable talking to you.

  First, take a deep breath. Ask yourself how you can use this situation to teach your children about sexuality and values.

- Don't feel you have to respond at all. Remember that sexual experimentation is normal, and that teenagers especially are entitled to a certain amount of privacy. Think about whether your child is really in any emotional, physical, or financial danger before you decide to intervene.

- Look beyond the obvious for your child's motivation. A child might be seeking additional information about sex, or experimenting—safely and vicariously—with new sex roles. If so, you might want to relate some of the worries and confusion you felt about sex when you were young. A child will be more comfortable and receptive to you if he no longer feels "weird."[12]

Begin by asking questions rather than by making statements. Listen to your child's side of the story so that you can help him better understand your position. A child who calls a telephone sex line, for example, may not understand who the women he's talking to are, or why they're talking that way, or how much it costs. Let him know that he's being exploited—at least financially—by the people running this type of business.

- Remember that sex education is a continuing process, not a single discussion. Don't worry if you handled this situation badly. You can always go back and try it again.

---

[12] There are times when this is the child's way of getting the parents' immediate attention and help for reasons totally unrelated to sexuality. But if that's the case, the child will probably be acting out in other ways as well.

7

Money, Jobs, and Career Aspirations

When it is a question of money, everybody is of the same religion.

—VOLTAIRE (1694–1778)

Money confuses children of all ages—and a good many adults as well. (I like to think that my own confusions are simply more sophisticated than they were a few decades ago.[1]) Jobs and money are highly complex concepts that tax the limits of a young child's skill at abstract thinking.

The confusion starts early and reflects the changes in children's cognitive abilities. To preschoolers, the fact that some small coins are worth more than larger ones, or that paper money the same size can have different values, goes against the logical structure they have painstakingly pieced together to make sense of their world.

---

[1] When I was four years old, my father took me to work with him for a day. I was fascinated. That evening my mother asked me what I thought about the things I'd seen. I told her how much I liked it, but that I was disappointed about one thing. My father never showed me where he *made* the money!

Checks, credit cards, and automatic teller machines further befuddle children, even throughout elementary school. While with a check there's an obvious trade of a piece of paper for goods, the link between that paper and a bank account is often missed by school-age children. Credit cards are even more confusing. After all, not only do you hand the cashier a piece of plastic, but you get it back along with your goods.[2] Automatic teller machines are, to many young eyes, simply magic. Insert a card and out comes "free" money.

By the time they reach adolescence, these confusions about money may not have cleared up. They may have simply risen to a higher plane. While teenagers understand the link between work and money, they are less clear on how their families spend the money they make, and how they should spend their own allowances and after-school earnings.

Also, one of the most important developmental tasks of adolescence is shifting from seeing yourself primarily as a member of your family to identifying more strongly with an outside social group of peers. That group may symbolically define itself by the things the members wear and own—both of which require decisions on how to acquire, save, and spend money.

In this chapter we'll explore those important connections, with an eye toward the developmental issues that influence teenagers' behavior with respect to money and work. As with most matters in adolescent development, it's useful to step back a few years to gain the most insight.

---

[2] A psychologist I interviewed told me how this point was driven home when she told her nine-year-old son that they couldn't afford to buy something he wanted. He suggested that she simply charge it to a credit card. When she explained that you still have to pay for something when you charge it, he was amazed. He'd never thought of that.

The Power of Money

Children are quick to sense the power and symbolic value of money. Long before they understand such concepts as saving and borrowing, they see the emotions their parents associate with those actions. They are also quick to notice their parents' different responses when they spend some of their allowance on a candy bar versus when they put it in a piggy bank.

While younger children often find frugality as distasteful as spinach, and some spend every quarter before it has a chance to get warm in their pockets, this should change by early adolescence. Their ability to think abstractly in sophisticated ways and to plan for the future is often reflected in how they spend their allowances and earnings.

Ideally, teenagers should be using what investment advisors call an asset-allocation strategy, which at this stage of their lives is more of a spending strategy. Their purchases should be less impulsive than they were a few years ago. They should be able to delay gratification sufficiently to save at least part of their income in order to pay for relatively expensive items.

Parents who try to dictate how their children handle their own money often find that those children spend recklessly as a way to rebel and to assert their independence. This can quickly turn into a vicious circle. The parents interpret their children's spending pattern as a sign of the need for even more rules and restrictions. The children respond by spending money even more inappropriately because they see what's happening as a battle over privacy and maturity, not finances.

According to Dr. Kenneth Doyle, a psychologist at the University of Minnesota who specializes in the psychology of money, those families who have the biggest problems with adolescents are those in which the parents believe in very strict controls on their children. While the intention is almost always good, they try to do it too much. He advises that the more important money is to you as a parent, the more important it is for you to give freer rein to your children.

While some children respond to this by becoming spendthrifts, others become too frugal. I'd be concerned about a thirteen-year-old who was saving most of her allowance for college. Such extreme behavior is almost always a reflection of the symbolic and emotional importance of money among the adults in her family. As with the teenager who immediately spends all of his cash, the compulsive saver has learned that such behavior gets her attention, even if it results in self-sacrifice or, in the case of a compulsive spender, punishment.

While some small amount of savings would be developmentally appropriate, it's important that a child this age learn how to spend most of her money on more immediate and short-term goals. She should be having fun while she explores the power and implications of money in her life.

Paying the Piper

Perhaps the most important lesson teenagers and younger children can learn about money—and the most effective method of teaching them how to save and spend it—is that of taking responsibility for their own financial decisions and actions. Ideally, adolescence should be a time for making mistakes because the consequences are usually minimal and lessons can be learned without too much pain.

Home and family offer the support needed to recover gracefully from those mistakes. Better a child should first learn at age sixteen, when he's living at home, what happens when you don't plan for basic expenses than that he should learn that painful lesson at college or when he's living in an apartment at age twenty-five.

A few years ago I interviewed the director of a consumer-credit counseling service, who said that many of the people he sees had parents who overprotected them or bailed them out of monetary problems when they were teenagers. The message these adolescents learned was not how to spend money wisely but that if they get into trouble, someone else will fix it for them. It is an expensive and emotionally draining misconception.[3]

Here are some things to bear in mind for helping teenagers learn to handle finances:

- Don't be concerned if a young adolescent "wastes" a lot of his money. What seems a poor decision to a parent can often be a valuable lesson for the child.

---

[3] There may be other emotional issues for the parents as well. A few weeks ago I sat in on an ongoing workshop for the parents of teenagers. Money was a recurring theme in their discussion. One (very well-to-do) mother was concerned that her two daughters, ages sixteen and seventeen, showed little responsibility in their financial affairs. When pressed, however, she said that whenever they wanted to buy something and didn't have the money, she gave it to them.

The more she talked, the more it became clear that despite her protestations, she craved her children's dependence on her and was reluctant to give that up. Since her teenagers were no longer physically dependent upon her, she had encouraged their financial dependence. Until the mother dealt with that underlying issue, she would continue to subtly sabotage her daughters' relationship with money and, in the long run, with her as well.

Let teenagers fritter away some of their money and see the consequences of that. Instead of lecturing them on their mistakes (which will cause them to focus their attention and emotions on you instead of their actions), help them explore what they did and talk about alternatives.

- Involve teenagers more in family finances, not only regarding major financial decisions (i.e., Can we afford to take a vacation this year? How can we pay for college tuition?) but also the nitty-gritty of family bookkeeping. I find it useful to have a teenager write (but not sign) many of the family checks and reconcile the account before letting him have his own checking account. (Be sure to check his addition!)

  This serves two purposes: It gives him practice in the mechanics of small-time bookkeeping, which is a prestigious adult-style responsibility that acknowledges his growth and maturity. Also, it helps him understand that you don't get to spend all of your income on stuff that's fun. The electric bills have to be paid before you can see if you have the cash to go to the movies.

- Expect your children's spending habits to reflect their stages of development. That will help you keep a sense of perspective, even if you disagree with how they're spending their money. For example, since adolescents are trying to define who they are, you should let them use their money to do that, even if you think the clothes and music they buy are obnoxious or just plain silly. (When in doubt, look at pictures of you when you were that age and ask yourself whether you'd still wear those clothes!)

- Be creative in helping them make decisions without dictating what they'll do. If your child wants you to buy him a pair of designer jeans, and you think it's wasteful, work out a compromise in which you both participate and get what you think is right. For example, offer to pay the price of a generic pair of jeans, and let your child pay the difference for the brand he covets. As one professor I spoke with put it, you buy the jeans but let him buy the logo.

- If you lend money to your child, make it a formal arrangement. While you don't have to pick up a fill-in-the-blanks legal document from the local office supply store, you should put the terms down on paper and have your child sign it.

    This isn't just because the sums are larger than they were a few years ago. It's an acknowledgment of your child's maturity and a recognition of his ability to plan ahead. I feel it's also a good idea to charge interest. While the actual amount of interest your child will pay on such small and short-term loans is trivial, it helps convey the idea that this isn't "free" money.

- Don't rush in with loans to help your child buy expensive items. Such acts of apparent kindness may backfire because teenagers haven't had the opportunity to reflect on what it means to spend that much of their income. The act of delaying a purchase by saving for it gives children a chance to think about how much they really want a particular item and to value it more when they do purchase it.

That means that if you want to chip in on an important item to help your child buy it, don't put up your money first. Instead, offer a matching grant so that you'll put in your money only after she's saved up enough for her share.

Where Credit Is Due

A generation ago, credit cards used to be solely the province of adults. A college student or even a recent graduate who applied for a card would be politely but firmly rejected, or asked to have a parent co-sign. Today, according to Mastercard International in New York, approximately 15 percent of all credit cards are held by people under the age of twenty-three.

For college students, the courtship ritual renews itself at the start of every semester. They find card applications already placed in shopping bags from the college bookstore, inserted into campus newspapers, and displayed on outdoor tables. Banks offer gifts just for filling out applications. The images in the brochures and advertisements reflect power, sophistication, and social acceptance—the very things that adolescents crave.

Perhaps the main reason why credit card companies are targeting adolescents is the tremendous brand loyalty people have to credit cards. Although a teenager who has a Visa card may switch banks after a few years, she's much less likely to switch to another brand of card.

For some adolescents, a credit card is a chance to learn about personal finance and establish a credit history. For others, it's a dangerous weapon prone to leaving self-inflicted financial wounds. By learning about credit while still in high school, and making the inevitable errors while the stakes are still low, teenagers can be better prepared for the increased responsibilities and opportunities that will be available to them once they graduate.

Those who don't get such early experience and practice can be shocked when they find out how quickly they can get into financial trouble. A friend of mine, who's the vice president of a major university, told me of a young student who had come to his office to request some money from the student loan fund. When he asked her why she needed the loan, she hemmed and hawed, but eventually admitted that she was so far behind in her payments on about twenty credit cards that collection agencies were calling her. Each card was at its credit limit, and she was unable to pay even the minimum amounts the creditors demanded. Her solution was to borrow more money. His solution was to hold what he called "a funeral." He asked her if she was prepared to cut up her credit cards while she sat there.[4] As tears streamed down her face, he handed her a pair of scissors and watched as she hesitantly began cutting.

Although the number of her cards and the size of her debt

---

[4] It's fascinating how many people (adolescents and adults alike) are reluctant to destroy a credit card, even if it's at its limit and therefore essentially useless. This shows how much of their self-esteem and even their identity is linked to possessing those pieces of plastic.

were unusual for someone that young, her plight and emotions are increasingly common. (The university vice president says he holds such funerals routinely.) One reason is the easy availability of credit cards, even to young people who have no credit history. The other is the images adolescents have of what credit means for the way they live, often culled from the thousands of television and print advertisements teenagers have seen for these cards, starting when they were in elementary school.

One danger of credit for adolescents is that it makes them feel like adults, perhaps before they're ready. They may feel that they're entitled to own certain expensive things before they've earned them (both literally and figuratively). This sense of entitlement comes at a time when adolescents are especially vulnerable to social pressures to buy things such as costly stereo systems or the right designer clothing. Most teenagers have difficulty setting priorities. They want to have it all, and to have it all now.

For older adolescents, going to college allows them a chance to reinvent themselves. They can shed the reputations that followed them through high school, and experiment with new images of who they are and how they should behave. One simple and tempting way to change their image is by buying things that they associate with glamour, power, popularity, and success.

In fact, college students who get into financial trouble often describe how they used credit cards to raise their self-esteem or to impress their friends and classmates. They may also use a credit card as a quick source of cash, offering to put a friend's meal or purchase on the card if the friend hands them the money. Many have no idea how much they've charged or how much interest they're paying on the debt.

Avoiding Credit Card Problems

Probably the most important thing you can do to prevent your children from getting into trouble with credit cards is to give them practice making financial decisions while they're still in high school.[5] I gave some suggestions for that earlier in this chapter. Here are a few other things you can try that can prevent, or help your child recover from, credit card problems:

- Consider debit and secured credit cards instead of traditional cards as a first step. These cards are especially good for teenagers who need practice and limits on their use of credit. With a debit card, all charges are automatically paid off by an interest-bearing account at a bank or other financial institution. Using a debit card is like writing a check against that account.

  With a secured account, your child maintains a savings account, and the amount on deposit deter-

---

[5] Make sure, however, that your expectations are realistic. A friend of mine who has a young teenage son was amazed when the boy's school wanted to teach his class about investing in the stock market. They had the students do some background research and "buy" a portfolio of stocks, which they tracked for a week before selling them. While their intentions were good, the results were a disaster. The behaviors they were modeling—buying and then quickly selling stocks—were completely inappropriate, since people who do such things in the real world are speculators and gamblers more than investors.

A much more realistic and useful lesson would have been learned had the class invested historically, i.e., "buying" a portfolio of stocks at the prices they'd been at ten years earlier based on information that had been available at that time, and then tracking how those stocks had performed relative to other economic variables (e.g. inflation, cost of living, Treasury-bill rates, etc.) over that ten-year period. A good public library will have all the resources you'd need to do this if you'd like to try it.

mines the card's credit limit. If the child doesn't pay the credit card bill, the bank can simply take the money out of the savings account.

- Work out a monthly budget with your children. This helps them anticipate expenses and adjust their spending accordingly. It's also good practice for when they're completely on their own. A monthly budget that's committed to paper makes it hard to deny reality and makes them more accountable.

- If your child has a financial crisis, listen before you act. Rushing in to solve the problem by paying off your child's debt isn't a good idea. Talk to your child to see how he perceives the nature and causes of the problem. Instead of being moralistic, which is likely to form a barrier to communication, help your child see what assumptions and behaviors led up to the problem, and what the consequences are.

  If you want to pay your child's bill to get him off the hook, it's also a good idea to take away or set stricter limits on the card, and to work out at least a partial repayment schedule, just as any other creditor would do. Be especially careful if trouble happens more than once. In fact, if your child's done this a few times, I suggest that you not bail him out at all. To do so would be like giving a drug to an addict. If you're going to pay his debts for him, understand the implications of your actions and what your child will learn from the experience.

Getting a First Job

Most adolescents look forward to getting their first job. It is a badge of their maturity and social worth, an important recognition of how they are changing. At their best, summer and after-school jobs provide teenagers with a chance to learn new skills, increase their self-confidence, and ease their transition to adulthood. At their worst, they offer little more than a menial wage in exchange for grueling, repetitive, unskilled labor that teaches adolescents nothing about themselves or the world of work.

The experience of finding and keeping a summer or after-school job should not be taken lightly. Researchers have found that those first few job experiences have more significant effects on a child's future work habits than many parents think.

Getting that first job outside the home can be a landmark for adolescents. It's an event that clearly differentiates them from their younger siblings and schoolmates. It is often the first formal acknowledgment by adults outside their family and school that something they know or can do has value in the adult world.

For a child who's having difficulty in school, a summer or part-time job may be an opportunity to succeed. It can help him feel good about himself, perhaps for the first time in a long while.

But the symbolic importance of this rite of passage, combined with teenagers' inexperience with employers and job interviews, means that for many adolescents, finding a first job can be confusing or even frightening. It puts their self-esteem on the line.

In addition, many teenagers have misconceptions about what prospective employers expect from them. When a colleague of mine recently spoke to a group of fifteen- and sixteen-year-olds about finding jobs, she found that some of them thought that they should be wearing a business suit and carrying a briefcase to an interview for an entry-level job. Others in the room thought they could show up as if they had just walked in off the beach.

Although it may feel as if you're doing your child a favor by using your influence to arrange for a job, that's often not the case. In many ways, the process of thinking about and searching for a job is at least as important to your child's self-concept as the work itself. Their sometimes awkward attempts to figure out where to apply, and the daydreaming about how they will spend the money from their paychecks, help teenagers try their new and more adult self-images on for size.

The teenager who finds his own job will usually have a much greater sense of accomplishment. If you arrange for a job for your child, that denies the child's need to try out his new sense of independence and competence. This doesn't mean you should be uninvolved. Rather, you should play a supporting role instead of taking the lead.

One way for teenagers to express their independence is the way they spend their paychecks. As with allowances, a paycheck allows teenagers to work on money-management skills under the guidance but not the control of their parents. For some teenagers, the sudden influx of money from a job gives them a distorted sense of personal economics. This misperception can have disastrous results once they can no longer count on their parents for room and board.

Long before a child begins to work, the family should discuss that child's plans for spending and saving earnings. This is also a good time to discuss the family budget, and whether a child will be expected to contribute toward living expenses or schooling. Studies in the late 1980s at the University of Michigan found that fewer than 10 percent of high school students who had jobs contributed more than half their paycheck toward family living expenses. Fewer than 13 percent saved half their earnings toward their education. More than 60 percent spent most of their money on discretionary items such as clothing, entertainment, and eating out.

Helping with the Job Hunt

If you're going to help your child find that important first job, here are some things you can do that take into account her normal emotional and developmental needs:

- Start looking early. The best time to look for a summer job is in the winter. That's also when you should begin helping your children clarify what they'd like to get out of a summer job. Talk about the people you know who might provide job leads. This may include school guidance counselors, parents' friends and coworkers, and social-service organizations. Remember that the best summer jobs are seldom advertised.

- Talk about the important parameters of a job well in advance. Many teenagers will judge a prospective job solely in terms of the hourly wage. Set guidelines about hours, location, and types of work ahead of time. If you try to do it after your child gets a job, you'll have much more difficulty setting limits.

  Keep in mind that when it comes to after-school

jobs, those studies at the Univeristy of Michigan have shown that high school students who work more than ten to fifteen hours per week during the school year are prone to a variety of problems, including a decrease in their academic performance and an increased likelihood that they will use cigarettes, alcohol, and other drugs. There is no single reason for those problems, but they appear to be related to the increased stress felt by children who try to work that many hours and go to school at the same time.

- Don't assume that a summer job has to be full-time. Forty hours a week may be overwhelming to a beginning worker. If your (and your child's) goal is to have a positive experience, working only a few days a week may go a long way in a first job.

- Expect your child to be nervous about the job search and the job interview. The amount of anxiety that your teenager shows, especially if you've discussed looking for a job well in advance, will often let you know if she is ready. A certain amount of nervousness is normal. But if she appears paralyzed by anxiety, she's probably not emotionally ready for the experience and the responsibilities.

- Review with your child what to expect during a job interview. This phase of the job search causes teenagers a great deal of anxiety. They are often extremely sensitive about how they come across to adults, and worry that the slightest flaw will prevent their obtaining a job.

But doing "pretend" or mock job interviews with your child may do more harm than good. The problem isn't the interview but the established parent-child relationship. In fact, your teenager may well be more nervous doing a mock interview with you than doing the real thing.

One good alternative, especially if your child has classmates who are in the same situation, is to arrange with other parents to do mock interviews with each other's children. Remember that you're interviewing for an entry-level job. Concentrate your questions on the basics. ("Why do you want this job?" "What experience do you have?" "Why should I hire you over the other applicants?") Ask them what questions they'd ask if they were the employer instead of the applicant.

• Make sure your child considers the possibility that she may not get the job. Job rejections can be especially upsetting to teenagers. Children this age—especially those who have been very successful at school—sometimes view being rejected for a job as a general statement about their worth. They may show this directly or indirectly, perhaps by describing the prospective employer as stupid or incompetent.

Help your child understand that everyone is turned down for jobs and that other employers won't know that your child has been rejected by someone else.

- Encourage your child to start building a résumé. Have your children tell their employers that one goal they have is to get a good letter of recommendation for future work. That sets the stage for a discussion about what's expected of their performance. And because the turnover of adults who supervise adolescents is very high, your children should request that letter of recommendation at the end of the summer, instead of waiting until the next year's job search.

The Ideal Job

From a developmental standpoint, the ideal summer or after-school job should provide adolescents with four things:

- They should have an opportunity to show that they can shoulder some responsibility
- They should be given a chance to learn and master new skills
- They should feel that their work and creativity are valued
- They should be able to work alongside adults and deal with people who are different from their neighbors and classmates

Unfortunately, most summer and after-school jobs obtained by teenagers offer few, if any, of those opportunities. Too often, their jobs require little training, are not creative, involve little responsibility, and isolate the workers with other teenagers. The sole reward they offer is the minimum wage. In fact, highly repetitive and mindless jobs like those in fast-food restaurants often make adolescents cynical about the world of adult work. The tasks are routine, unchallenging, and regimented. The teenage workers feel, and in fact are, completely replaceable.

Despite those problems, certain aspects of almost any summer job can help children mature. They get experience seeing situations from other people's perspectives. What's it like to wait on someone rather than to be waited on yourself? How does it feel to be nice to total strangers all day, even if you don't want to be? They also see how their behavior affects other people. (If you come to school five minutes late, only you will suffer. But if you're five minutes late to your job, someone else may have to cover for you, or you may have to work for someone else who's late.)

When you're talking to your teenager about jobs, remember that the best jobs often pay nothing at all. Volunteer work for nonprofit organizations and social service agencies usually offer adolescents a much more valuable set of experiences than most entry-level summer jobs. Many volunteer positions require training and the acquisition of new skills. The work is more varied, and the volunteers usually feel more valued by the organizations than those who work for the minimum wage. Volunteer work also often puts adolescents in touch with people from a wide range of social and cultural backgrounds. This experience can help them become more sensitive to other people's problems.

Volunteer work can also pay off financially in the long-term more than a typical entry-level job. Employers of college-age workers are generally more impressed by a work history that shows how the teenagers accepted responsibility and followed through on projects than one that shows that she can grill a hamburger or operate a cash register.

If your teenager needs money, and you can afford it, you might even consider paying out of your own pocket a child who is working at a volunteer job. It's an investment both in your child's future and in the quality of life in your community.

Problems on the Job

Attitudes about work are one key factor in how successful an adolescent is on the job. While some embrace almost any job, others have a sense of entitlement. They don't believe they should have to start at the bottom or do things they don't want to do. Many teenagers are fired two or three times before they really begin to understand what work is about.[6]

In fact, being fired from a job can be what educators refer to as a "teachable moment." Helping a teenager learn and make the most of what happened can require considerable tact and insight. Blaming your child for losing the job will simply make him resentful of and angry at you. Trying to reassure a child by saying that getting

---

[6] As with other financial issues, it may be better that they go through this as adolescents than as young adults. Several years ago I hired a new college graduate to work for me. After only a few months I had to fire her because she refused to do the work that needed to be done. The underlying problem was one of attitude: She was only interested in doing a task when it was new. Once she mastered a skill, she wanted to move on to something else.

In essence she treated the job as if it were school and I was supposed to spend my time as her teacher. (She forgot that, unlike school, I was paying her, not the other way around!) I understand that she went through several other jobs very quickly after she left our business, probably for the same reasons. It would have been better for everyone if she had learned those lessons when she was a teenager instead of waiting until she was twenty-one.

fired is no big deal may backfire, for the child may interpret that as a confirmation that both he and his work aren't important.

Instead, use the incident as a trigger for a discussion in which your child explores not only what happened but his feelings about it as well. What did he do wrong? What did he do right? Were there any signs that this might happen? Why did the boss fire him? What should he do differently the next time?

You can expect your child to try to assign the blame to someone or something else—his supervisor hated him or the system's unfair. Let him vent those feelings, but gently redirect the discussion to his own behavior, since that's the only thing he can control.

Entering the Workforce

You shouldn't be surprised if your child has difficulty adjusting to her first job. She's probably going to be confused and fearful, although she may express those unwanted emotions as anger and arrogance. Here are some things you can do to help:

- Let your child spend some time with you at your job. Even one or two brief visits—after hours if necessary—can give your child more realistic expectations of what he or she will be doing. Many young adolescents have little idea of what their parents really do at work. Explain to your child not only what you do but why you think it's important.

- During the summer, talk to your child about what she is learning about the world of work. Gently correct her misconceptions. Some adolescents take on too much responsibility and have to learn when to ask for help. Others need to be encouraged to stand up for themselves.

You may hear teenagers describe work as something they do to earn money so that they can later do something they like. They don't see anything of intrinsic value in their jobs. Because of that, they may come to the conclusion that they shouldn't expect to feel good about their work.

- If your child wants to quit, listen closely. Often all your child needs is to ventilate emotions to someone who won't be critical. This situation also offers her the opportunity to see the situation from her employer's point of view.

  Talk about what led up to her feelings. Describe the times when you felt the same way, and what you learned from your experiences. Then ask your child what she would do if she were the supervisor and had to deal with someone like her.

Trying on Careers for Size

Many adolescents announce their future careers with the same blind passion with which they fall in love. They shun practicality in favor of idealized images and wishful thinking. Parents who hear their teenagers say that they want to become full-time poets, sculptors, philosophers, or professional football players are likely to cringe at the odds against success. We worry that such unrealistic choices will leave our children emotionally distraught and financially dependent upon us for a long time.

But adolescents tend not to pay attention to those odds. Such shortsightedness is normal. It is a way for them to toy with images of themselves as self-sufficient adults, to try on new roles and see how they feel. That's why their attachments to careers are often as fleeting and fickle as their love lives, and potentially as volatile. It's normal for a fifteen-year-old who's announced with conviction that she wants to become a lawyer to change her mind a few weeks later and say that she'll definitely work as an engineer.

Athough parents usually encourage high aspirations and self-confidence in their children, many become nervous if adolescents cling to the idea that they will become rock stars, professional basketball players, or Hollywood idols. Often, the more parents try to bring their children to their senses, the more desperately those teenagers insist that they are bound for such unrealistic glory. ("It may be a one-in-a-million chance, Mom, but someone has to be that one. Why shouldn't it be me!")

One reason is that television gives children daily looks at celebrities and often minimizes the hard work and luck that underlie their achievements. This is especially true for sports figures, who appear to be making fortunes simply by having fun and endorsing products.[7]

---

[7] According to a college coach I interviewed, each year there are approximately twenty-five thousand varsity basketball players at colleges and universities in the United States. Each year, NBA teams hire about fifty new players. Although you might think that means that every varsity player has about a one-in-five-hundred chance of getting a professional contract, that's not true, since many of the players hired by the teams have been out of school for several years, or have been playing in the minor leagues or in other countries.

Another reason adolescents may harbor unrealistic career aspirations is that these are the years when social status takes on an overwhelming importance. They focus on the adulation and fame instead of the realities of the job.

Not all adolescent career dreams are focused on fame and money. A man I interviewed for a newspaper column who had been the head of personnel at the New York Zoological Society[8] told me that he used to receive several hundred letters a month from adolescents who wanted to become zookeepers or wildlife biologists. A recurring theme in those letters was the unrealistic image many of them had of the job—that they'd be feeding and playing with wild animals all day.

In response, he started a series of workshops for high school students on choosing a career. For the first time, many of those students realized that they needed a background in mathematics and science, as well as a college degree, to be a zookeeper. It was also a chance for them to see the relevance of what they were studying in school to work in the real world.

Occasionally, however, the reasons for a prospective career choice are more cryptic. The zoo administrator confessed that until he was thirteen years old, he'd wanted a job with the New York City Sanitation Department. He'd heard that they stopped work in the early afternoon, and figured that a job with them meant he'd have the time to go to major-league baseball games.

---

[8] When I was growing up, we simply called it the Bronx Zoo.

Channeling Career Aspirations

Even though you know his dream is unrealistic, don't rush in to correct your tone-deaf fourteen-year-old who insists he'll be a Broadway star. Let him enjoy the fantasy for a while. Such dreams are part of normal childhood, and show that he's at least thinking about his future. Let him use those dreams to search for the boundaries of who he is and what he can accomplish.

Instead, give him information that will help him formulate plans that include reasonable alternatives if his original dreams prove to be out of reach. Here are some specific ideas:

- Ask questions, but don't jump in too soon with advice. Show respect for your child's thinking, even if you disagree with the conclusion. The process of examining the alternatives is what's really important. One rule of thumb, taught to me by a psychologist I know, is that for every caution or warning you feel you must state to your child, say two positive things about his prospective career choice. Even if you don't think a career as a music composer makes sense, you can talk about how rewarding it would feel to see your child's compositions in print and to hear them being performed.

- Help your child analyze his career aspirations. If he wants to be a professional actor, ask him what he likes about the job.[9] Remember that the process of answering that question is more important than his actual response.

Many adolescents who say they want a particular career have given little thought as to why. Help your teenager see additional ways he can do the things he likes. If he says he enjoys performing in front of a crowd, talk about other careers that use some of the same skills, such as teaching or sales.

- Help your child explore other careers within the same field. Point out the number of jobs listed in the credits of a movie or television program. Help your child think about the different people who are involved professionally in sports without playing them, such as agents, coaches, trainers, referees, reporters, and publicists. Talk about how, for example, even though he's interested in a career as a painter, he might also study computer graphics as a

---

[9] When I worked as a television reporter, I would routinely spend time with college students who hoped to get a job in broadcasting once they graduated. These students would spend a day or two with reporters as "ride-alongs" so that they could see what it was like. While most of them were realistic about their chances and willing to put in the hard work it took, I remember one nineteen-year-old who had stars in her eyes.

All she wanted to do, she told me, was be a television reporter or maybe a news anchor or a talk show host. (That should have tipped me off!) I mentioned that the odds against getting a job as a television reporter were quite high, and that she could help herself by gaining experience in other forms of journalism by writing for newspapers and magazines.

Oh, no, she said. She only wanted television. When I pressed her on why, she told me, "Well, I don't like to write, and I know that in television you don't really have to write."

I had to restrain myself from physically throwing her out of the station. During a typical eight- to ten-hour day as a television reporter, I would spend less than four *minutes* in front of the camera. The vast majority of my time was spent gathering information and writing. Yet she noticed none of that.

way of earning a living while he paints, and doing it in a way that's related to what he loves to do best.

- Encourage your child to get information from people in the business that interests him. It's usually best if your child makes at least some of these arrangements on his own. That way he'll pay more attention to the information than if you arrange for the interviews. If your fifteen-year-old can't talk directly to a professional athlete or movie star, suggest that he approach a college coach or drama teacher for advice.

During these interviews, your child should find out what the professional tennis player was able to do on the court at fifteen, or what grades the surgeon was getting and what courses she took when she was in high school. This information will help your child decide if his goals are realistic, and what he'll have to start doing now to reach them.

8

On to College . . . or Perhaps Not

*The studious class are their own victims; they are thin
and pale, their feet are cold, their heads are hot.*
—RALPH WALDO EMERSON (1802–1882)

Although the focus of this chapter is college, I'd also encourage
those parents whose children won't be enrolling in higher education to read it. I've used college as a context for exploring some
of the important developmental issues of late adolescence—issues
that must be addressed even if your child isn't attending school.
Because of the growing numbers of teenagers who move from
high school directly or quickly to a college or vocational school
of some sort, I've used the college experience to help put these
issues in perspective.

For many high school seniors, the fall semester is a time to
fill out college applications, peruse course catalogs and glossy
brochures, and watch promotional videotapes. It is a daunting
and emotionally charged task for both the students and their parents, and is best begun with some introspection.

The first step in evaluating a college should be for the student to evaluate himself:

- What are my strengths and weaknesses, both in academics and elsewhere? Am I more interested in science than in liberal arts? Am I easily distracted by extracurricular activities?
- What kinds of learning environments allow me to do my best work? Am I more comfortable in a small school, or would that be too confining? Would a large school feel overwhelming? Do I like to control my own schedule, or do I do better if my day-to-day activities are highly structured?
- With what types of people do I like to associate? Am I more likely to feel a part of a school in which intercollegiate athletics are emphasized or minimized? Do I find fraternities and the like attractive or aversive? Do I like being with people who are mostly like me, or would I like to meet and live with people who are different?

College advisers and admissions officers warn that many students apply to schools for the wrong reasons, ranging from the number of stars they receive in guidebooks to the presence of world-renowned faculty members. Students may avoid schools that are not household names or whose tuitions seem out of reach.

It can be dangerous to put too much faith in books and articles that purport to tell you the "100 Best Colleges and Universities" or that provide some similar rank-ordering of schools. The reviewers' criteria and your own may be substantially different. The number-one school on the list may be a much poorer choice for your child than number eighty-five or even many of the thousands of other schools that didn't make that particular cut.[1]

While it may sound prestigious to have a Nobel laureate or two on the faculty, advisers caution that in many schools, these faculty members have little if any interaction with undergraduates—and occasionally don't have much to do with graduate students, either.[2]

Also, the "sticker price" of tuition, like that of most new cars, often has very little to do with what the student eventually pays. The most expensive private colleges and universities usually have the highest "discount rates." That's because it's these schools that tend to have the largest endowments and, hence, the most money for financial aid. Four years at an "expensive" Ivy League university may actually cost less than four years an an "inexpensive" small private college, because the financial-aid package the university offers may be substantially greater.

That's why you shouldn't rule out any college or university because of its stated tuition. Instead, ask to speak to a financial-aid officer, or the financial-aid counseling service at each school, in order to get an estimate of the amount and types of aid (loans, on-campus jobs, and grants, for example) that they're likely to offer.

---

[1] While there are numerous guidebooks to colleges and universities published each year, I suggest you and your teenagers also read another book, which gives an insider's perspective on college admissions and related issues: *The University: An Owner's Manual,* by Henry Rosovsky (W. W. Norton & Co., 1990). Dr. Rosovsky was, for many years, the dean of the faculty of arts and sciences at Harvard University.

[2] When I was in graduate school, there were several world-class faculty members in our department. I was lucky enough to have one of them, who was a Regent's Professor of psychology, psychiatry, philosophy, and law (note that he was a full professor in the medical school without having a medical degree and a full professor in the law school without having a law degree), for a weekly two-hour seminar in which I was one of fewer than a dozen students. The seminar lasted the entire year. At the end of that time, and despite the small size of the class, I doubt that he knew the names of half the students. It wasn't one of his priorities.

Although many admissions officers are reluctant to admit it, financial-aid offerings are often open to negotiation—especially if your child's an exceptionally good student or meets other important criteria for that school. If your child is offered a better financial-aid package from school A, but would really like to attend school B, there's nothing wrong with going back to the admissions office and asking them (politely and respectfully, of course) whether they'll match the other offer. After all, you have nothing to lose.

Many parents enjoy the process of choosing a college with their children. It gives us a chance to relive our own experiences, or to do something we never did when we were younger. However, counselors at high schools emphasize that while parents should be actively involved in the college selection and application process, the fundamental decisions and responsibilities should be left to the students.[3]

This can lead to some conflicts at home, since many adolescents feel ambivalent about the upcoming important changes in their lives. Applying to college can become a symbol for many of those changes. If parents push too hard or try to control that important series of decisions, teenagers will focus their emotions and energies on struggling against their parents' wishes instead of examining themselves, the schools and their future.

One rule of thumb is that parents should back off but not bow out. Let your child know that you're available as a willing and enthusiastic resource, but let her control and be responsible for the mechanics of applying to college. Your child should be the one to make the telephone call to the admissions office to set up

---

[3] One high school counselor I interviewed described how parents would routinely come to his office and talk about how "we" were going to college.

the interview and the tour, and should be the first one to reach the desk and extend her hand to the admissions officer.

It's also a good idea for prospective applicants to write to the admissions office of any school they're seriously considering and to ask for specific information about a department or area they are interested in. How the school responds—with a personal letter or telephone call from a faculty member, a specialized and relevant brochure, a general and largely irrelevant brochure, or by ignoring the request entirely—will say a lot about the school's responsiveness to the students it enrolls.

Finally, trust your instincts. If your child visits a campus and feels uncomfortable, it's probably not a good match, no matter how prestigious or popular the school is. Her gut reaction is important. Many of life's important decisions are choices of the heart, not just choices of the mind.

Cutting Through the Hype

A few years ago I was asked by my undergraduate alma mater (Oberlin College) to write and produce a pair of videotapes to introduce prospective applicants, new students, and their families to what the school was like. I began by reviewing similar tapes produced by a variety of colleges and universities. It was, to put it bluntly, a mind-numbing experience.

A few were the slick products of advertising agencies and public relations firms. These tended to look pretty but say little of import about the schools. Another small group were student-produced and idiosyncratic, but more honest. The bulk of the videotapes, however, were so generic that the name of one school could be replaced with that of another, and it would retain much of its accuracy.

Typically, these videotapes would start with a helicopter shot of the campus, usually taken in the fall when the leaves were changing color. A sonorous "Johnny Goodvoice" announcer would talk in voice-over about how "Wupperman College, founded in 1883, is one of the finest undergraduate institutions in the country (or region, or state)." The tape would then dissolve to a classroom shot of neatly lined-up rows of students listening to a lecture by an archetypal bearded professor as the actor droned on about the quality of instruction.

Soon it would dissolve to a sequence in which we see a female professor in her office, feigning surprise and graciously welcoming a student who had knocked on her door. The disembodied voice takes this cue to emphasize the individual attention students receive. Additional sequences showed the athletic facilities and dormitories.

After seeing a dozen of these, I couldn't recall which school was good at what or had which special facilities. But what was most striking was that I had actually learned very little about the truly distinguishing characteristics and flavors of the schools from their videotapes.[4]

It's always important to take college-recruitment materials, whether they're videotapes, glossy brochures, or even

---

[4] I'm proud to say that when we produced the videotapes for Oberlin, we used a very different approach. We shot them as if they were PBS documentaries. There was no off-camera announcer. The only people we heard from were the students and a few faculty members and administrators, who told of their own opportunities, experiences, and passions. That painted a more honest and, quite frankly, a much more exciting picture of what it might be like to attend school there.

the course catalog, with a large grain of salt.[5] Paying too much attention to such materials may not only lure you and your child to a school that's inappropriate, it may cause you to reject a school that might have been a good fit.

Probably the most important thing that students and, if possible, parents should do is visit any school they are seriously considering. But simply taking a tour and nervously sitting through a thirty-minute interview with an admissions officer probably won't say very much about what it's really like to be a student there. Here are some other things you can do:

- Ask questions that tell you about issues that aren't mentioned in the brochures. For insight into what dormitory life is like, find out how many students move off campus after their freshman year. (If there's a predictable mass exodus, that's not a good sign.) Ask about the proportion of introductory courses taught by graduate students. Find out the percentage of students who graduate within five years. (If there are a lot of dropouts, ask why.)

- Walk around campus and talk to people after the tour. Your child should try to meet with graduates

---

[5] I must admit to inadvertently contributing to this. In addition to my work at Harvard Medical School, I was for several years affiliated with a child and family research and public-policy institute at a large state university about six hundred miles from where I live. As part of that work, I was granted an unpaid faculty appointment as an adjunct full professor in one of the academic departments on campus. (The reasons have to do with university politics.)

Since receiving that unpaid appointment nearly four years ago, I have not met with a single student or faculty member in that department. In fact, I've never even been inside their building. While the other faculty members and I knew from the beginning that this would be the case, odds are that entering students did not. They may have assumed that since my name was listed in the course catalog and faculty directory, they'd be able to take a course from me.

of his high school who attend the college to find out what the transition was like. Don't be shy about stopping students or faculty members to get their perspective on the school.

- Try to spend a night in a dormitory. Many schools will arrange for this if you give them sufficient notice. At the very least, try to sit in on an introductory course in a subject you enjoy and arrange to eat a meal in a dining hall. While there, talk to the students about both the good and bad things that surprised them after they arrived at the school.

- Look at campus bulletin boards and pick up the student newspaper. The newspaper will tell you what the important issues are on campus. Bulletin boards give you a flavor of campus life. If all the notices are about houses for rent and requests for weekend rides to other cities, that tells you a lot about how unhappy students are at that school.

Taking a Break After High School

A young woman at Brown University told me in an interview a few years ago that she had decided during her senior year of high school that she needed a break from academia before going off to college. While most of her graduating high school classmates spent their next year taking introductory courses in biology, sociology, foreign languages, and English composition in college, this woman created her own classroom for studying the world.

During the fifteen months after her senior year of high school she studied birds of prey with wildlife biologists in the mountains of Nevada and Utah, worked to improve small farms in Arkansas and Mexico, built houses with Cree Indians in northern Ontario, and wrote educational materials for the Vermont Youth Conservation Corps. Most of the projects provided her with room and board in exchange for her labor. Two provided transportation, and one gave her a small stipend.

When I interviewed her father, he said that the experience was much less expensive than a year of college. He admitted that one reason he supported his daughter's adventure was that he had wanted to do something similar when he'd been her age, but his parents were afraid that if he took a year off, he'd never go back to school.[6]

But the benefits were more than financial. The young woman, who was finishing her sophomore year when I spoke with her, was focusing her studies on developing countries. She said that her experiences made her appreciate college more than she would have if she had gone there directly. In her words, "The year away from school made me more enthusiastic about learning because I realized how much I needed to learn."

A growing number of students are taking sabbaticals between high school and college. For most, it's the first time they've taken

---

[6] This is a common concern, of course. According to Cornelius Bull, a former preparatory school headmaster and the president of the Center for Interim Programs in Cambridge, Massachusetts, which helps students plan such volunteer adventures, that fear is totally unfounded. This makes sense, since those students who are unmotivated to attend college will find a way to leave even if they attend immediately after high school. I'll deal with the issue of preventing dropouts later in this chapter.

responsibility for planning their own schedules for more than a summer. It's a chance to experience another culture and, perhaps, to learn a new language.[7]

A year away from the classroom is an especially good option for those students who are academically talented but emotionally burned out. It gives them a chance to pause and regroup. For some teenagers who have been having difficulty in school, a year doing something else gives them a chance to build their confidence by being successful and more independent. Lastly, for those children—usually boys—who are late bloomers emotionally and physically, the extra year before college gives them a chance to grow up.

One reason high school seniors often cite for taking a year off is that they didn't get into the college of their choice. But this by itself isn't an especially good reason for spending time out of school. A year of real-world experience will seldom make up for poor high school grades. A more reasonable approach would be for the adolescent to spend the next year getting the best grades he could at another college and then trying to transfer to the school he prefers.

Similarly, wanting to take a year off from school to "find yourself" or to "travel around the country" may be a setup for a disappointing experience. The vagueness of the plans indicate that the teenager has been avoiding facing some of the real issues in this important step toward adulthood and independence.

---

[7] The college counseling office at Phillips Academy, a preparatory school in Andover, Massachusetts, surveyed several hundred of its alumni who had graduated between 1975 and 1985 and who had taken time off between high school and college. It found that every single one of the respondents stated that, if given the opportunity, they would repeat the experience.

Arranging for an Interim Program

The one thing that all successful interim programs have in common is lots of planning. The research and planning process, which includes a thorough review of what the student wants to get out of the year, can be as valuable to a teenager as the program itself. College advisers, reference books on volunteer work, and independent consultants can help point students and their parents in the right direction.

Here are some other things to keep in mind:

- Your child should fill out all college and financial-aid forms during his senior year as if he were going there directly, even if he wants to take time off. There are several reasons for this. First, it's administratively much simpler to apply to college while you're still in high school. It also gives your child a chance to change his mind in the spring if the interim program doesn't seem to be working out.

- Work out a budget for the year. While some interim programs are as costly as a year in Princeton, others are free or may even leave your child with a little spending money. There can be striking differences in cost, even between similar programs.

- Research the programs thoroughly. Don't just believe the brochures. Ask the people running the program to give you names of past participants. Ask those people to give you the names of others who may have viewed the program differently. Ask consulting services if they receive commissions from any program, since that may bias their recommendations.

- Have your child explain to the college he wishes to attend (and that has accepted him) what he'll be doing for the year and why. Most colleges will routinely grant accepted students a one-year deferral of admission if there's a valid reason.

The Emotions of the Freshman Year

A friend of mine once described in vivid detail how he felt during his first few days as a freshman violin major at a large university. He'd won much acclaim as a high school musician in his hometown and was sure that college would be only a way station on his fast track to an international concert career. Then he heard the other violin students practicing.

"There was the terrible moment when I feared that the admissions office had made a mistake, and I would soon receive a second letter asking me to leave under the cover of darkness to spare everyone the embarrassment," said my friend.

No such letter came, of course. In fact, my friend is now a vice president of that same university. Yet his feelings exemplified what are commonplace emotions during the first few months of the freshman year.[8]

---

[8] I still remember a meeting the first night of freshman orientation at my all-male dormitory at Oberlin College. The first thing the senior resident asked of the forty or so of us who were sitting in the room eyeing each other was for a show of hands of all those present who had been president of the student council or editor of the school newspaper, yearbook, or literary magazine in high school. Much to our surprise (and his amusement), every single hand in the room went up. "Gentleman," he said, "welcome to Oberlin!"

The first year of college is punctuated by feelings of panic and incompetence. Psychologists and university administrators say that for most students, the fears are predictable and may help them make the transition to adulthood.

As I've said earlier, the early teenage years are a time for children to experiment with separating from their parents. By taking more control of their social lives and by earning some of their own money, they can test what it's like to be more independent. Throughout this early testing, however, their parents are still nearby, providing a safety net.

The first few months at college give late adolescents a chance to fly without that net, with all the excitement and terror that freedom naturally provides. During freshman orientation, the students may appear uncomfortable around their parents and ask them to leave quickly, or at least walk on the other side of campus. They are sure their anxieties are abnormal and that they must impress their new classmates with how mature and independent they really are. They're champing at the bit to give this form of adulthood a try. But they're also feeling ambivalent, lonely, and perhaps even a bit abandoned.

For the first time, many adolescents must make entirely their own decisions about how they will spend their time, when they will eat, when (and if) they will sleep, and what they will study. They must go from the top of high school to the bottom of a new hierarchy. And they must find new friends among strangers.

In some ways, it's like moving to a foreign country. There's a new landscape, a new culture, and a new language full of acronyms and nicknames. Even the food is nothing like it was at home.

While entering freshmen may express their anxieties directly, many send their messages obliquely. They may withdraw or show a great deal of bravado. Their phone calls home may contain complaints about the workload ("I have to read four books and write two papers this week!") or fanciful descriptions of the school's food ("We call it mystery meat, Mom. Someone said it was owl.")

There is something of a paradox in those complaints. By describing the cramped dorm rooms and institutional cuisine, they are reassuring themselves that they are mature enough to handle the challenges they face. By complaining about the heavy workload, they are letting you know that they are getting their (and your) money's worth out of the tuition.

Before you become too upset with what your child is saying, remember that it's actually a compliment. He's letting you know that he trusts you enough and feels secure enough in his relationship to believe that you won't reject him for having such emotions. It shows you've done a good job.

Responding to a Panicked Call

University administrators can sometimes predict which adolescents will have a lot of trouble adjusting to college life. The students who have the most difficulty are often those who've had the fewest experiences with people who are different from them.

But even the most worldly freshman may sometimes feel overwhelmed. If you get a panicked phone call, here are some things to keep in mind:

- Say less than you used to say. A main developmental task for children this age is learning to handle things

- Compare your agendas for the visit. Many parents and children have different expectations about what they will do and how much time they will spend together during the weekend. If you discuss this ahead of time, you can avoid unnecessary feelings of intrusion or disappointment.

- Don't expect your child to take on the role of host throughout the visit. Plan the times you will be apart as carefully as you plan the times you will be together. Ask your child to suggest things you might do or see by yourselves while on campus.

- Bring cookies, newspaper clippings from home, and news about old friends. These reminders of and symbolic connections with home are always appreciated.

- Don't expect your children to be very organized, even if they were that way at home. Most college students don't plan ahead. You shouldn't be surprised if your child hasn't made a dinner reservation at a nice restaurant, for example. After all, such forethought isn't usually needed in his new day-to-day life.

- Remember that children who move away from home want to distance themselves from certain aspects of their past. Assiduously avoid embarrassing your child by talking about painful memories or telling embarrassing stories. They may cut too close for comfort.

- Try not to fall back into old roles, especially with respect to the new people in your child's life. Asking to speak with your child's teachers, for example, may be seen by your child as a slap in the face. After all, that's what you do with high school students, not college students.

- Don't comment on the state of your child's room, even if it's a mess. It's so easy to fall into that well-practiced role of expressing your concern. Instead, treat her as you would a new neighbor and let her show you her world.

Handling Potential Dropouts

Of the thousands of adolescents who will be going off to college in the next year, a disturbing number will not graduate. For many of those students, the freshman year will be a watershed. Within days of starting their first classes, they will find themselves facing rigorous academic and social challenges unlike anything they have ever experienced. All too often, their response to these challenges will be to drop out of school.

According to research by Dr. Vincent Tinto, a professor of education at Syracuse University, only about 62 percent of students who start a four-year program will finish their degree within ten years. Almost half of those who drop out will do so within the first year of college. The proportion of students who drop out of college varies widely from school to school. In general, the more selective the college is, the higher the graduation rate.

According to researchers who study these attrition rates, many of those decisions to leave school for good are preventable. Often the solution, they say, is to provide more counseling and other support services to students early in the freshman year. But parents also need to understand what will be happening to their college-bound children and how to help them complete their degrees.

Few academic problems crop up during the first month or two of school. (The problems may be there, although they're not yet visible before midterm exams.) Administrators say that most early concerns of freshmen stem from homesickness and mismatches between the child and the school.

Those mismatches are more likely to be social or cultural than academic. For example, students from small high schools sometimes have difficulty adapting to large urban campuses. Freshmen may feel intimidated by professors.[10] Many entering students feel isolated and, at the same time, are unaware that a lot of their classmates feel the same.

It's a good idea to encourage students to speak to professors after class instead of simply sitting passively in the classroom. This helps make the professors more real as people and helps students feel more a part of their own education.

Also, becoming involved with at least one extracurricular ac-

---

[10] Many adolescents—even those in college who are comfortable tackling philosophy or physics—still have difficulty imagining that their professors have fully formed lives outside the classroom. Let me give you an example. A friend of mine used to teach an introductory psychology course at the University of California at Irvine. One afternoon, when he was shopping at a local supermarket, he noticed that one of his students was working as a cashier. He wheeled his cart full of food over to her cash register and said hello. As she looked from his face to the cart and back to him again, she gasped and cried out in surprise, "You eat!"

tivity in the first semester is a way of building relationships with other students and breaking through feelings of isolation. Campus work-study programs are another way of integrating students into campus life and preventing dropouts.

Freshmen who are feeling overwhelmed by college often worry that they have failed their parents. This is especially true if the child is the first in the family to go to college. They carry more of a symbolic burden on their shoulders. Such feelings of failure only compound the problem, of course, for those students believe they are the only ones who are having difficulty coping with the changes. They don't understand that their confusion is a normal part of growing up.

That's why it helps if parents describe their own worries and confusions when they were the age of their children. Knowing that such feelings are normal can lend tremendous reassurance and remove many of their concerns about being a total failure.

A colleague of mine, who's a senior administrator at a large university and has spoken with many anxious and confused students, has developed a wonderful approach to offering these adolescents a new perspective. "I never tell them that they'll get over their feelings," he says. "They never will. But their questions will become more polished and less fearful."

Listening to a Student's Fears

Few students—and fewer parents—prepare for college with the intention of not graduating. That's one reason why dropping out is such an emotional topic. But if your child tells you that she's thinking of quitting school, there are some things you can do to help her evaluate whether that's the best solution to what's bothering her.

- Remember that a child's announcement that she's leaving school may be more of a test of your reaction than a firm decision on her part. Listen to her reasons without belittling her fears or quickly suggesting alternatives. Be nonjudgmental and allow your child to ventilate her feelings.

- Don't speak in platitudes, such as "These are the best years of your life." After all, both of you know that with any luck at all they won't be. Besides, it doesn't help a student to hear pat phrases like that. They're both depressing and threatening to a teenager who's feeling overwhelmed.

- Ask your child about her fears, even if she hasn't spoken of them. It's often useful to describe some of your own fears when you made a major change in your life, such as starting college, beginning a new job, or moving to a new neighborhood. This helps reassure her that her worries are normal, and that she's still capable and healthy.

- Don't offer solutions. This is difficult for many parents (myself included). Instead, after listening to her, reaffirm your faith in her abilities and refer her to the student counseling center. Let her know that everyone needs support at times.

- Don't encourage your child to come home. Even
  though it may feel like a kind offer at the time, encouraging your child to do that is usually a mistake.
  It reinforces her feelings of failure, undermines her
  struggle for independence, and may simply prolong
  the problem because it avoids her having to deal
  with the underlying issues.

  Instead, while you're exploring alternatives with
  your child and encouraging her to seek support from
  the college or university, remind her that if she de-
  cides to stay in school, she'll always be able to leave
  at a later time. Sometimes simply knowing that the
  option will still be there give her the strength and
  reassurance she needs to plow on.

9

Letting Go

How selfhood begins with a walking away,
And love is proved in the letting go.

— CECIL DAY-LEWIS (1904–1972)

I've often heard parenthood described as a job in which your ultimate goal is to put yourself out of business. Nothing could be further from the truth. If we are to stay with that metaphor, a more appropriate image is that your job description as a parent constantly shifts. To succeed, both you and your children must learn to change your relationship as you each grow and face new challenges and responsibilities.

This growth is sometimes more difficult for parents than for our children. After all, we can remember their diapers and their first steps, while they cannot. We can look beneath their beards and makeup, their attitudes and accomplishments, and see the children at the core of these young adults. We hold these images and memories dear to our hearts.

I'd like to take a few pages to talk about the future—the relationship between parents and their adult children. My reason for including this admittedly cursory discussion here is that many of the difficulties in parent-child communication that occur between young adults and their parents can be traced to problems during the teenage years. By recognizing that, you may be able to improve your future relationship with your children by focusing on some issues during their adolescence.

Moving Back Home

A prime example of this often occurs when a young adult, often a college graduate, moves back home because she's emotionally unprepared to be off on her own. Few of these children (and few of their parents) recognize that this is the reason for their return. Instead they focus on the tight job market for recent graduates or the price of rental apartments. But further investigation and introspection will often show that the real reasons lie elsewhere, and that the problem could probably have been prevented.

For example, a young woman I spoke with at a friend's Fourth of July party told me how excited she had been by her first taste of independence from her parents when she was a college freshman. She spent the following summer living at her parents' home, and described it as a nightmare. She swore to herself that she would never live with her parents again. She was wrong. At age twenty-four, and with a bachelor's degree in both psychology and biology, she was once again living in her parents' home.

She is not alone. The proportion of young adults who are supported by their parents reached a thirty-year high in the mid 1980s—the latest figures available from the U.S. Census. There's no evidence that it has decreased significantly if at all over the past decade. This reverses a trend, starting after World War II, toward more young adults living independently.

According to 1984 Census Bureau figures, 53 percent of men and 32 percent of women between the ages of twenty and twenty-four were living with or having their living expenses paid by their parents. This had increased from 40 percent and 26 percent respectively a decade earlier.

But researchers say that those figures underestimate the true situation. Dr. Allan Schnaiberg, a sociologist at Northwestern University who has been studying families in which adult children return home, noticed that when he would speak to groups of parents about this phenomenon, often more than 80 percent of the audience would nod their heads as if this had happened in their families.

While some of this might be accounted for by the self-selection of who would attend such a lecture, Dr. Schnaiberg realized that the fundamental problem with the Census Bureau data lay in the way they were collected. The government's figures were like a snapshot: They only showed the total at any given moment. A much larger proportion of young adults move into or out of their parents' homes. They just don't do it all at once.

The sharpest rise has been among middle-class and upper-middle-class young adults in the United States and Canada, since that is the group that was most likely to have lived away from home a few decades ago. Among less affluent North American families and in many European countries, the number of young adults who expect to live with their parents has been significantly higher. That difference between Americans and Europeans, say sociologists, reflects the relative shortage of housing and jobs in many European countries, the increasing average age of marriage over the past few decades, and the cultural expectation that living at home is what a young adult will do.

The reasons for the increasing number of so-called "boomerang kids" in this country are unclear. While simple explanations, such as the delay in age of marriage since the 1950s, permissive parenting styles, or an increase in both taxes and the price of housing relative to income, may explain some of the cases, they don't seem to account for this sharp a rise, say sociologists. They do, however, offer some insight as to which children are most likely to come back home as adults.

According to Phyllis Jackson Stegal, a Seattle psychologist who has studied this phenomenon, many of those young adults who return home have never learned how to handle and bounce back from failure. Their parents tended to bail them out of trouble rather than let them find solutions for themselves. She also found that many of these young adults have a distorted view of money.

The young woman I'd met at the party admitted to fitting both these descriptions. Although she'd been looking for a job in counseling or personnel, it had been a halfhearted effort. While large corporations could offer her a career path, their starting salaries for such jobs were less than she was making as a waitress. She was also reluctant to start at the bottom. "I'm used to a certain way of life," she told me. "I don't like that I won't be able to buy what I want. I'd only be able to buy what I need."

Her parents, who had paid her tuition and expenses during college, had recently told her that she would have to find her own apartment and pay all her living expenses by the end of the summer. It was a difficult decision for them to make. Much to their surprise, their daughter was grateful.

"I'm glad that they set that deadline, because they've never said anything like that to me," the young woman said. "They've always been there as a buffer. They never let me fall hard. Now I have to take charge of my own life."

Guidelines for a Returning Young Adult

We shouldn't be too quick to condemn young adults who return home or to dread the experience. In some families it can be mutually beneficial—when each generation can give the other the extra help it needs.

But even when that isn't the case, it's better to think of the situation as a temporary setback that can actually help strengthen your relationship with your child. Some very good things can come from this time back home. It's an opportunity for young adults to repair some childhood wounds and complete some of their unfinished business of growing up.

One of the most helpful things parents can do for a young adult who has come home again is to work out a written contract that outlines everyone's responsibilities and sets limits on how long your child may stay. Although writing out a contract may appear impersonal and perhaps even cold-blooded, it emphasizes that as parents you will now have different expectations of your child than when she was younger. It also prevents both generations from later saying,

"I didn't know you meant that," or "I never thought you felt that way."

Here are some suggestions for the content of such a contract. All of these assume that your child is able to work, and has not returned because of a serious illness or a similar situation.

- Although the young adult should suggest a time limit for the stay, the final decision should rest with the family. She should also let her parents know what types of emotional support she wants—and doesn't want. Too much mothering or fatherly advice can add strain to a situation that's often already uncomfortable.

- As part of that contract, the young adult should pay rent and contribute toward food. For the first month or so, she may have to do extra work around the house to earn her keep. Her financial contributions should increase during her stay. Keep in mind that your goal is to replicate the real world at home. Paying for your own room and board is one aspect of adulthood that makes it different from childhood.

- The contract should recognize that the parents have no control over what the child eats, how she dresses, the hours she keeps, or her sexual activity, since those are decisions she should make as an adult. When those behaviors disturb the family, however, then it's something other members of that family have the right to restrict or comment on.

- If you're providing financial support to your child, set a schedule for tapering it off. You may, however, have to give her some extra money when she leaves your home to help with the up-front expenses of renting an apartment.

- Allow your child to make mistakes and recover from those mistakes by herself. Ideally you should have done this when she was much younger, of course. Still, it's better to start late than never.

- Fulfilling this contract at home is very similar to meeting the expectations of an employer or landlord. As the contract approaches its expiration, point out to your child her success at fulfilling her part of the deal. Seeing that success can sometimes give the young adult more confidence in her ability to be independent.

- Unless there are extraordinary circumstances, such as a serious illness, don't extend the deadline for moving out. When the time is up, she simply has to go. Parents who set limits get these young adults back on their feet much more quickly than parents who don't. Setting limits is a loving thing to do.

When Your Child's in Trouble

There's no question what you should do as a parent if your nine-year-old gets into serious trouble. You step in and take charge,

protecting your child from any dangerous or painful consequences. Your actions are not as clear, however, if the child in
trouble is nineteen or twenty-nine. Although your love for your
children may be the same when they reach young adulthood,
your responsibilities and obligations are quite different.

When either generation fails to acknowledge those changes, a
relatively minor family crisis can leave everyone involved feeling
angry and hurt. Major but recoverable problems, such as a
child's drug abuse, impending divorce, or possible bankruptcy,
can turn into disasters.

A psychologist I interviewed for a newspaper column described this situation vividly, although with a bit of hyperbole.
Helping your child when she's an adult, he said, is like walking
through a minefield years after a war. You can trigger emotional
explosions left over from when the child was younger unless both
of you have dealt with and defused those issues.

The most important issues revolve around competence and
independence—the focus of many of the battles between adolescents and their parents. When a parent refuses to recognize a
child's development, or a young adult hesitates at becoming self-
reliant, the parent-child relationship can become frozen in time.[1]

When parents who haven't adjusted to their child's adulthood
sense that their child is in trouble, they may rush in with unwanted or inappropriate help. Two false beliefs underlie their
missteps. They act as if they still have control over their child, so
they do what they would have done fifteen or twenty years ear-

---

[1] One psychologist told me that she was treating a sixty-three-year-old woman who was upset that
her eighty-seven-year-old mother was still meddling in her affairs. It was as if the younger woman
was still a teenager living at home.

lier. And they act as if their child's life belongs to them and is still their responsibility.

This is not to say that parents should simply steer clear of their adult children when they sense trouble. The real problem is deciding when you should intervene and when you should let them weather the storm by themselves. One rule of thumb is to get involved when the problem directly affects either you or any dependent children. Are people calling you to collect your child's debts? Is your son telephoning you from jail to ask for bail money? Is your daughter's behavior affecting the health or safety of your grandchildren? If one of these or something like them is the case, you should become involved.

But if you question whether it's a serious problem, or if the situation doesn't affect you or a child who may need your protection, don't intervene. If you're upset because your child's in a career that you don't like, but your child is happy, that's your problem, not your child's.

Offering Help

If you do decide to intervene in your adult children's problems, here are some suggestions for avoiding mistakes:

- Don't rush in and take over. That's likely to compound the problem, since it allows your children to focus on what *you* are doing instead of what *they* are doing. It also puts both you and your children in a relationship and power struggle that's more appropriate for a parent and a nine-year-old than for two or more adults.

- Take your time and plan your strategy. Let them know that you appreciate their points of view and their feelings. Be sure to acknowledge their adulthood and their ultimate responsibility for their own actions—both getting into trouble and getting out of it.

- Don't expect your observations and offers of help to be welcomed—at least at first. It's often difficult for adults in serious trouble to admit that they have problems, especially when a parent points those problems out. Recognize that in the stress of the situation, your child may treat you as a meddler, intruder, or controller.

- Mobilize other family members to help. If you don't do that, your child may think that you're the only one who sees a problem. This is especially true if your child is addicted to alcohol or drugs. Also, don't let your child come between you and your spouse. Form a united front. Talk to each other and work out an agreement before you take any action with your child.

- Give your child an opportunity to suggest solutions. This shows your respect for your child's maturity and ultimate responsibility. Set clear limits on the type and amount of help, if any, that you can give. Will you co-sign a bank loan, pay for eight sessions of family therapy, or simply help your child find an attorney? Such limits are also a sign that you recognize that your relationship is now different.

Competition

Competition is one way parents and children define and solidify their relationship with one another. A game of checkers between a five-year-old girl and her father is inherently unfair. Its value is mostly symbolic, for it allows children to test new roles and skills in relative safety. It's less frightening for a child to fail among people who love her than among strangers. A father who chooses not to win every time is giving the child important messages that he is not all-powerful and that is is all right for her to be better than her parents.

Competition can become a problem, however, when either generation has the feeling that the other is tripping it up. Those trips are most likely to occur when children are adolescents or young adults. The balance of power between the generations is becoming more equal. No longer can the parents simply decide whether to lose the game.

For some, watching our children excel can be tremendously exciting. For others, watching that same success can be surprisingly upsetting. Often those parents describe themselves as only wanting the best for their children. Yet when those children surpass them as adults, it can sometimes make them feel like failures.

When Dr. Ronald Levant was the director of the Fatherhood Project at Boston University, he would repeatedly hear stories from successful men in their thirties and forties who were disappointed by how little acknowledgment and recognition they received from their fathers.

Related research by Dr. Peter Davis, the director of the Division for Family Business Studies at the Wharton School of Business at the University of Pennsylvania, supports that. He found that parents, especially if they were the founders of a family business, didn't want to be outshone by their adult children who were working in that business. They tended to become angry when their children discussed their accomplishments, and to dismiss the value of their children's education—especially if it was an education that those parents did not have.

Such feelings need not be confined to family businesses, of course. Dr. Levant described an interview he'd had with a young man who was a very successful stockbroker and who had spent his career analyzing investments. He complained that his father wouldn't listen to him. When his father wanted to invest in stocks, he would ask his old friends or even total strangers for advice. The father had lost money; the son felt hurt that he'd been ignored.

The source of this type of snub is more likely to be the father's insecurity than any distrust of his grown-up child's knowledge and skills. Going to an old friend for stock information is a way of denying that he's not in the same league as his son anymore—at least in this area. It's a way for the father to maintain his self-image.

But the adult children, because of their emotional involvement, tend to misinterpret what's going on. They focus on their own hurt feelings rather than on their parents' fears. The pattern repeats itself.

Ending Painful Competition

A first step toward resolving uneasy feelings of competitiveness with your children involves wading through the complex and often conflicting emotions that accompany the problem. Here are some suggestions for opening up communication in this situation:

- Ask yourself about the relationship between your children's accomplishments and your own goals for yourself, especially when you were their age. Feelings of competition are often particularly acute when a child succeeds at something that the parents would like to have accomplished themselves.

  From the other perspective, adult children may feel guilty when they do better than their parents, because they've knocked those parents off their pedestal. That guilt may make it more difficult for children to talk with their parents about their lives.

- Ask yourself what your feelings of competition really represent. Are they born of fear and insecurity over how you compare with your children? If so, whom do you see making such a judgment? Why is that person's opinion so important to you?

  Are your emotions tinged with sadness over your own accomplishments? If that's the case, what your children are doing isn't really the issue.

- Look for activities from your past that you can do with your children, and which you both used to enjoy without feeling competitive. One man who participated in the Fatherhood Project at Boston College described how he and his father broke out of the rut of destructive competitiveness when they went deep-sea fishing together. It was a sport that the two of them had looked forward to immensely when he was a boy. Doing it together as adults helped them renew their bonds.

An Ending and a Beginning

It's difficult to write a conclusion to a book on a topic for which there is no conclusion. While it's possible to define when adolescence begins, there is no single biological or emotional marker of the start of adulthood. That is part of the magic and fascination of child development.

Although your children, who have been so dependent upon you throughout their lives, may now move away (perhaps several times!), mere distance does not sever the ties that bind you forever as parent and child. It's important to view those ties as connections rather than constraints; guides, not absolutes.

Rather than indulge in platitudes, I would like to end on a personal note. As I write this, my wife and I have become the foster parents of a seventeen-year-old boy, the son of a colleague and friend in Romania. Flavius joined our family a few months ago. I use that phrase advisedly, for he will be linked to us for the rest of our lives. He is on the brink of adulthood, testing his independence as he attends school seven time zones away from his mother, father, brother, and grandmother—the people who had nurtured and supported him in person until now.

A week or so after he moved in, I was struck by a feeling that seemed oddly familiar. When he first came to this country, he knew no one outside our family. Of necessity, we controlled his schedule for those first days as he made the adjustment to life in a strange new world. But soon he began to talk of some friends he had made on the tennis court. They were people we had not met, and who were occupying what to us were unseen areas of his life.

It reminded me of the first time my son, Michael, when he was three years old, came home from preschool and talked about his new friends. No more was my young child merely an extension of me. He had a social life that involved children I had never met. He was becoming independent.

So it was with Flavius, although because of his age he achieved in days what had taken Michael years. He had asserted his independence from us. While it marked a change in our relationship, it was a time for celebration. We had the confidence that he could make the transition. He knew that he was acceptable in his new country.

And so we all changed as he took this important step toward adulthood. We look forward to the continuing shifts in how we relate to one another, knowing that the core of mutual confidence, love, and respect will remain the same.

Index

Abusive relationships, 117, 118–122
accidents, car, 72, 73, 131, 132, 135,
    136
Addictive Behaviors Research Center,
    133–134
adolescence, *see* teenagers
adoption, 47–51
    emotional issues of, 50–51
Adoptive Families of America, 47*n*
adult children:
    financial support of, 202–203, 207,
        210
    moving back home by, 200,
        202–207
    offering help to, 209–210
    parental competition and, 211–214
    in trouble, 207–210
aggression, 60
Alan Guttmacher Institute, 141–142,
    141*n*
alcohol use or abuse, 7, 61, 73, 84,
    110, 113, 127–128, 133
    of adult children, 210
    aerobic exercise and, 136–137
    binge drinking as, 133
    driving and, 131, 132, 135, 136
    homosexuality and, 145
    meditation and, 137
    parenting advice on, 127, 131, 132,
        134–137
    parties and, 136
    part-time jobs and, 165
    role models and, 133
    stress and, 136
allowances, 151, 152
American Society of Plastic and Re-
    constructive Surgeons, 18
anorexia, 14

anxiety:
    of college freshmen, 189–190
    job search and, 165
    shyness and, 90–91
appearance:
    cosmetic surgery and, 17–21
    fashion statements and, 8–9, 33–34
    parents as models of, 16
    parent-child conflicts over, 31–34
    self-image and, 1–4, 14
    underlying issues and, 8
    young children and, 2, 19
asset-allocation strategy, 152
asthma, 21, 22
attractiveness:
    alcohol and, 134, 134*n*
    idealized female image of, 2, 5–6
    objective measures of beauty and, 2
    smoking and, 138*n*, 139
    weight and, 10
autonomy, 9, 24–25, 29, 32, 56, 57,
    58, 114, 115, 130
awkwardness, 1–2, 3, 15
    alcohol and, 133
    in social situations, 58, 91

Bacon, Francis, 52
beauty, cultural standard of, 2, 5–6
bedtime, 65–66
behaviors:
    risky, 127–149
    setting limits on, 41, 80, 207
Block, Jack, 128–129, 129*n*
body image, 1–3, 9
    distortion of, 14
    eating disorders and, 14–16
    of idealized female, 5–6

body image (*continued*)
  preoccupation with, 1–4
  teens and, 155
"boomerang kids," 204
boys:
  appearance and, 2
  eleven-year-olds, 4
  puberty in, 4–7
  relationship breakups and, 123–124
  shyness and, 91
  smoking and, 138
  thirteen-year-olds, 1–2, 52
  time off before college for, 186
Boyz N the Hood (film), 80
Breakfast Club, The (film), 80
breakups, relationship, 122–124
  parenting advice on, 124–126
breasts, development of, 3, 4, 5
Brooks-Gunn, Jeanne, 5
Brown University, 184
budgets, 161
  first jobs and, 163
bulimia, 14
Bull, Cornelius, 185*n*

Car accidents, 72, 73, 131, 132, 135, 136
career aspirations, 171–173
  interviews and, 176
  parenting advice on, 174–176, 209
Census Bureau, U.S., 202–203
Center for Interim Programs, 185*n*
Centers for Disease Control, U.S., 141–142
changes in teenagers:
  during college, 180, 193
  coping with, 3–4
  discipline and, 38–43
  first jobs and, 162
  parent-child relationships and, 26, 27, 201
  physical, 1–7, 15, 32, 52

psychosocial, 7
runaways and, 68
chin augmentations, 18, 19
chronic illness, 21–25
cigarettes, *see* smoking, cigarette
clothing, 78, 81, 87, 90
  peer rejection and, 88
  sexy, 101
  see also appearance
clumsiness, 1–2, 4
cognitive skills, 53
college(s), 115, 169*n*, 175*n*, 177–200
  admission deferral policies of, 188
  applications for, 177, 180
  dropouts, 183, 185*n*, 196–200
  evaluation of, 177–179
  freshman year of, 188–192
  moving back home after, 202–210
  one-year sabbatical before, 184–186, 188
  problems adjusting to, 190
  professors, 197
  selection of, 180, 183–184
  tours of, 181, 183
  visiting teens at, 192–196
college-recruitment materials:
  course catalogs, 177, 183
  cutting through hype of, 181–184
  glossy brochures, 177, 181, 182
  promotional videotapes, 177, 181–183
communication, parent-child, 26–51
  adoption issues and, 47–51
  on appearance, 31–34
  conflicts in, 27–31, 53, 69
  disciplining in, 38–43
  productive arguing in, 29–31
  religion and, 43–47
  sharing experiences as, 4, 4*n*, 9, 16, 103, 144, 171, 199
  strengthening of, 205
  threats to run away and, 69
  see also talking with teenagers

competitions, parental, 211–214
    resolutions of, 212–214
confidence, gaining of, 92–93
conflicts, parent-child communication
    and, 27–31, 53, 169
    about appearance, 31–34
    see also communication, parent-
        child
consciousness, altered states of, 127,
    130, 132, 136
contracts, for living at home,
    205–207
cosmetic surgery, 17–21
counseling, professional, 61–62, 122,
    129–130, 199
credit cards:
    avoiding problems with, 160–161
    children's views of, 151
    college students and, 157, 159
    self-esteem and, 158n, 159
    tearing up, 158, 158n

Dates, dating, 98–126
    abusive relationships and, 117–122
    alcohol and, 134, 134n
    early, 99–100
    first, 105–109
    lack of interest in, 102, 103, 104, 106
    mixed-group, 104, 105
    one-on-one, 105, 106
    parenting advice on, 108–109,
        116–118
    parents' experiences with love and,
        144
    problem, 113–115
    timing of, 101–104
Davis, Peter, 211
Day, Doris, 106
Day-Lewis, Cecil, 201
Dead Poets Society (film), 80
debit cards, 160
    see also money
decision making, 67, 83
    alcohol and, 131, 132–134

financial, 153–154, 155, 160
    mistakes in, 86
    on schedule planning, 186, 189
    teaching of, 84–86
defects, physical, 8
dependency, 56
depression, 59–62, 79n, 82
    see also emotional development
development, physical, 5–6, 7, 7n
    identification with groups and, 31,
        151
dieting, eating disorders and, 14–16
DiFranza, Joseph R., 138
disabilities, teenagers with, 21–25
discipline, 38–43
Doyle, Kenneth, 152–153
    see also alcohol use or abuse
driver's license, driving, 71–76, 113
    drinking and, 131, 132, 135, 136
    status from, 71
dropouts, college, 196–200
drug use or abuse, 7, 79, 82–83, 84,
        84n, 118, 127–132
    adult children and, 208
    part-time jobs and, 165
    predictors of, 129–130
    "safe," 131
    signs of, 130

Eating disorders, 4, 14–16
Elkind, David, 100
embarrassment, 56–59, 82
    alcohol use and, 131, 134
    appearance as source of, 3
    of parents over teen's weight, 11
    public, 59
    teenagers with disabilities and, 21
    young children and, 56–57
Emerson, Ralph Waldo, 177
emotional development, 22, 31,
        52–76, 167–169
    of burned-out students, 186
    parenting advice on, 54–55
emotional problems, 61, 61n

emotions:
  acknowledging intensity of, 8
  confused, 17
  food and, 10–11
  freshman year at college and,
    188–190
  see also specific emotions
entitlements, work and, 169

Failure, handling of, 204
family businesses, 212
fashion statements, 8–9, 31–34, 78,
  81, 86, 90
  popularity and, 87
Fatherhood Project, 211, 213
features, facial, see appearance
Feindler, Eva, 119
fighting, parent-teen, 27–32, 33
  see also communication, parent-
    child
finances, see money
financial aid, 179–180
Fisher, Seymour, 2
Flavius (foster child), 214–215
flirting, sexual harassment vs., 96
freshman year at college, 188–198
  adjusting to, 190–193
  dropouts and, 197–198
  parents' visits during, 192–196
  see also college
friends, friendships, 53, 77–82
  chronically ill teens and, 23
  as destructive relationships, 79–82
  experimentation with, 77–79
  harmful influence of, 77, 78
  inappropriate, resistance to, 79–86,
    114–115
  isolation from, 60, 92
  with nondrinkers, 135
  with nonsmokers, 137
  parenting advice on forming of,
    79–82, 89–90
  parents' disapproval of, 79–82
  popularity vs., 87

savior role in, 118, 120
secretive, 79
understanding of, 79–82
see also peer pressures

Gangs, membership in, 78n, 83
Garfinkel, Barry, 59
"garlic symptoms," 59
girls:
  abusive relationships and, 119
  attractiveness and, 2, 6–7
  eating disorders and, 14n
  fighting and, 7
  fourteen-year-olds, 7
  preteen, 98–99
  puberty and, 4–7
  relationship breakups and, 122–123
  seventeen-year-olds, 106
  shyness and, 91
  smoking and, 138
  soap operas and, 147
  social aggressiveness in, 99n
  ten- to twelve-year-olds, 4, 7
  ten-year-olds, 7
Girls, Inc., 90
"going steady," 99, 102
Green, Arthur H., 119
groups, affiliation with, 78, 83, 151
growth spurts, 1–2, 15, 52
Guttmacher, Alan, Institute, 141–142,
  141n

Habits:
  money-spending, 155
  work, first jobs and, 162
harassment, sexual, see sexual
    harassment
hashish, 127
Health and Human Services, U.S. De-
    partment of, 67
Heathers (film), 80
Herzog, David, 14n
Hill, Charles T., 123–124
home, moving back to, 205–210

homesickness, college students and, 193
homework, 37, 65
homosexuality, 145
Hudson, Rock, 106–107

Identity, credit cards and, 158*n*
independence, 9, 22, 26, 27, 32, 55, 77, 114, 130
    adult children and, 208
    college and, 189
    dating and, 115
    financial, 154, 154*n*
    paychecks and, 163
"in" group, 87
Institute for Social Research, 127
Insurance Institute for Highway Safety, 74
interim program, 184–188
intervening, for adult children, 209–210
interviews:
    college, 181, 183
    job, 166, 176
intimacy, 23, 144

Janus, Mark-David, 68
jobs, 162–164, 167–169
    attitudes and, 169, 169*n*
    entering the workforce and, 170–171
    entry-level, 163, 166, 168
    getting fired from, 169–170
    hunting for, 164–167
    ideal, 167–169
    mock interviews and, 166
    part-time, 162, 165, 167–169
    problems with, 169–171
    quitting of, 171
    setting parameters for, 164, 168
    success and, 169
    summer, 167, 168, 170

volunteer work as, 168–169, 185*n*, 187
Johnston, Lloyd D., 137
Journal of the American Medical Association, 73
"Just say no!," 82, 84, 84*n*, 128

Kidney disease, 21
Klesges, Robert C., 138*n*
Koocher, Gerald P., 22–23
Kutner, Michael, 215

Levant, Ronald, 211, 212
limits, setting of, 41, 80, 207
looks, *see* appearance
Loretta Young Show, The (TV show), 107*n*

Marijuana, 127, 129
Marlatt, Alan, 133, 136
mass media:
    alcohol use and, 133, 134, 135
    celebrities portrayed in, 172
    cigarette ads in, 135, 140
    credit card ads in, 159
    incidents of harassment and, 95
    sex and, 144, 147
    teenagers portrayed in, 5–6, 15, 77, 95, 99, 100–101, 106
MasterCard International, 157
meditation, 137
menarche, 4, 5, 7
Mencken, H. L., 77
Merchant of Venice, The (Shakespeare), 127
Michigan, University of, 163, 165
money, 150–157
    asset-allocation strategy of, 152
    career aspirations and, 173
    children and, 150–153
    discretionary items and, 164
    distorted view of, 204
    first jobs and, 163

for living expenses, 206
parenting advice on, 153–157
as symbol, 152–153
Monroe, Marilyn, 10
motivation, rewards as, 34–38
moving out, 62–67
music, 78, 81

Name-calling, 31, 93, 94
National Commission on Adolescent
    Sexual Health (1994–1995),
    141, 141*n*
New York Times, The, 109
New York Zoological Society, 173,
    173*n*
nonconformity, 78

Oberlin College, 181, 182*n,* 188*n*
"onion symptoms," 59
Orbuch, Terri L., 122
overweight, 9–13
    rejection and, 88
    see also weight

Parent-child communication, *see* com-
    munication, parent-child
parenting advice:
    on abusive relationships, 120–122
    on adult children living at home,
        205–207
    on alcohol use or abuse, 131, 132,
        134–137
    on apologizing, 42
    on arguments, 29–31
    on career aspirations, 174–176, 209
    on chronically ill teenagers, 24–25
    on college selection, 183–184
    on competition with adult children,
        212–214
    on conflicts over appearance, 33–34
    on cosmetic surgery, 19–21
    on credit card problems, 160–161
    on dating, 101–104, 108–109

on decision making and resisting so-
    cial pressures, 84–86, 114–115
on developing a sense of responsibil-
    ity, 37–38
on discipline, 40–43
on domineering behavior, 83
on dropping out of college,
    198–199
on drug abuse, 130–132
on eating disorders, 15–16
on emotional tensions, 54–55
on feelings of embarrassment,
    58–59
on first jobs, 164–167, 170–171
on friendships, 89–90
on gaining perspective on appear-
    ance, 8–9
on helping adult children with prob-
    lems, 209–210
on helping teens gain confidence,
    92–93
on identifying clinical depression,
    61–62
on inappropriate friendships, 79–82
on interim programs before college,
    187–188
on issues of adoption, 50–51
on letting children go, 67, 201–215
on losing weight, 12–13
on money, 153–157
on moving out, 65–67
on popularity, 89–90
on problem dates, 116–118
on prom night, 111–113
on relationship breakups, 124–126
on religious challenges, 45–47
on responding to college freshman's
    panicked calls, 190–192
on rewards of unpleasant tasks,
    37–38
on safe driving, 75–76
on sex, talking about, 144–146
on sexual harassment, 95–97
on sexually explicit materials,
    148–149

parenting advice (continued)
  sharing stories as, 4, 4n, 9, 16, 103, 144, 171, 195, 199
  on shyness, 92–93
  on smoking, 139–140
  on talking about sex, 144–146
  on talking about underlying issues, 8, 15
  on teaching, not punishing, 40–43
  on teens' physical changes, 3–4
  on threats of running away, 69–71
  on underlying issues, talking about, 8, 15
  on visiting teens at college, 192–196
parties, alcohol and, 136
peer pressures, 2, 17, 21, 24, 77, 78, 82–86, 101
  alcohol use and, 135
  drug use and, 130
  harmful relationships and, 77
  popularity and, 86–90
  prom night and, 111, 112
  puberty and, 5
  resistance of, 79–86, 114–115
  sexual activity and, 143
  sexual harassment and, 94–95
  social acceptance and, 2, 17, 21, 24, 101
  spending money as, 159
  see also friends, friendships
Phillips Academy, 186n
physical changes, 1–4
popularity, 86–90
pornography, 146–147
power struggles:
  offering help and, 209
  parents' control and, 192
  weight loss as, 12
pregnancies, 141, 142
preschoolers, money and, 150–151
preteens, 67, 70, 98–99
Princeton University, 187
privacy:
  money issues and, 152
  as sign of drug abuse, 130

privileges, 41, 75
proms, 109–111
  expenses of, 110–111
  parenting advice on preparing for, 111–113
psychosocial problems, 7
puberty, 1, 2–7, 15
  arrested development of, 4
  early onset of, 7, 7n
  timing of, 4–7
punishment:
  compulsive spending and, 153
  discipline vs., 38–40
  parenting advice on, 40–43

Race, smoking and, 137
rebellion:
  cigarettes and, 140
  domineering parents and, 83
  fashion statements as, 78, 81, 90
  food selection as, 12
  religion and, 26, 43–47
  see also abusive relationships
rejections, job, 166
religion, challenges to, 26, 43–47
  parents' values and, 78
responsibility(ies):
  developing sense of, 37–38
  increasing of, 41
  for money, 153–154
  for schedule planning, 186, 189
  for teenagers with disabilities, 22–23, 25
  for weight loss, 9, 12
résumés, 167
rewards, as motivation, 34–38
rhinoplasties, 18, 19, 21
Richards, Maryse, 15
Rosen, James C., 6–7
Rosovsky, Henry, 179n
runaways, 63, 67–71
  chronic, 68

first-time, 68
  threats of, 69–71

Schnaiberg, Allan, 203
self-consciousness phase, 3, 15
self-deprecation, 17
self-esteem:
  alcohol use and, 134
  credit cards and, 158n, 159
  first job and, 162
  low, 13, 92, 119
  organized activities and, 82, 90
self-evaluation, college selection and,
  178
self-image:
  appearance and, 1–4, 14
  of fathers, 212
  of parents, 191
  temporary, 192–193
self-perceptions, 1–4
self-reliance, 208
"self-talk," negative, 91, 92–93
senior proms, see proms
separation, leaving home as, 62–71, 189
sex education, 149
sexual abuse, 119, 136n
sexual activity, 7, 8, 28, 48–49, 79, 83,
  84n, 101, 110, 127, 140–144
  of adult children, 206
  parental advice on, 144–146
  responsibility and, 143
  unprotected, 131
sexual harassment, 93–97
  flirting vs., 96
  mass media and, 95–96
  parenting advice on, 95–97
  school policy on, 96–97
  teasing vs., 94
sexually explicit material, 146–149
sexually transmitted diseases, 141, 142
Shakespeare, William, 127
shyness, 90–93
  alcohol use and, 131, 132
  problems resulting from, 91–92

smoking, cigarette, 127, 128, 137–140
  part-time jobs and, 165
social acceptance, alcohol and, 133
social aggressiveness, 99n
social development, group identifica-
  tion and, 31, 151
social pressures, see peer pressures
social rejection, 88–90, 101
social withdrawal, 92, 129
Some Kind of Wonderful (film), 80
status, social, 71, 173
Stegal, Phyllis Jackson, 204
Steinberg, Laurence, 105–116
stress, alcohol use for, 136
substance abuse, see alcohol use or
  abuse; drug use or abuse
suicide, 60, 61, 79n
  homosexuality and, 145

Talking with teenagers:
  on abusive relationships, 121–122
  on adoption, 50
  on dates' behaviors, 117
  on differences of opinions, 46–47
  on drinking and driving, 136
  on drugs and alcohol, 132, 136
  on fears about college, 199
  on harassment, 96
  on intimacy, 144
  on job parameters, 168
  patience and, 55
  on "saving" troubled friends, 118,
    120
  on sexual orientation, 145
  sharing experiences and, 4, 4n, 9,
    16, 103, 144, 171, 195, 199
  on threatening to run away, 67–68
  underlying issues and, 8
  on values, 131
  see also communication, parent-
    child
tasks, unpleasant, teenagers' performance of, 34–38
"teachable moments," 169